The PRACTICE of PRAISE

The PRACTICE of PRAISE

C. H. Spurgeon

Whitaker House

THE PRACTICE OF PRAISE

ISBN: 0-88368-296-6
Printed in the United States of America
Copyright © 1995 by Whitaker House

Whitaker House
30 Hunt Valley Circle
New Kensington, PA 15068

4 5 6 7 8 9 10 11 12 13/ 06 05 04 03 02 01 00 99 98 97

Contents

Chapter 1

The Philosophy of Abundant Praise

"They shall abundantly utter the memory of thy great goodness, and shall sing of thy righteousness."
—Psalm 145:7

This is called "David's Psalm of Praise." You will see all through it that he has a strong desire for God to be greatly magnified. Hence he uses a variety of expressions and repeats himself in his holy zeal. Run your eye down the psalm and notice such words as these: *"I will extol thee...I will bless thy name"* (v. 1), *"Every day will I bless thee; and I will praise thy name forever and ever"* (v. 2), *"Great is the LORD, and greatly to be praised"* (v. 3), *"One generation shall praise thy works to another"* (v. 4), *"I will speak of the glorious honor of thy majesty"* (v. 5), *"Men shall speak of the might of thy terrible acts"* (v. 6), and other similar words, down to the last verse: *"My mouth shall speak the praise of the LORD: and let all flesh bless his holy name forever and ever"* (v. 21).

David is not content with declaring that Jehovah is worthy of praise, or with pleading that His praise ought to be felt in the heart, but he will have it publicly spoken of, openly declared, plainly uttered, and joyfully proclaimed in song. The inspired psalmist, moved by the Holy Ghost, calls upon all flesh and all the works of God to sound forth the praises of the Most High. Will we not respond to the call?

In outlining his design for praise, David speaks in verse five of the majesty of God, the glorious King. His eye had seemed to be dazzled by the glorious splendor of that august throne, so he cries out, *"I will speak of the glorious honor of thy majesty."* Then he ponders the power of that throne of majesty and of the force with which its just decrees are carried out, and so in verse six he exclaims, *"Men shall speak of the might of thy terrible acts, and I will declare thy greatness."* Here he speaks in brief both as to the majesty and the might of the dread Almighty. However, when he turns his thoughts to the divine goodness, he enlarges and uses words which indicate the stress which he lays upon his subject and his desire to linger over it. *"They shall abundantly utter the memory of thy great goodness."*

Now, our desire is that we also may praise and magnify the name of the infinite Jehovah without restraint or limit, and may especially have our hearts enlarged and our mouths opened wide to speak abundantly of His great goodness. In all of the congregation of believers may the text become true: *"They shall abundantly utter the memory of thy great goodness."* Also having uttered it in plain speech, may we all rise a step higher and sing of His righteousness with glad music.

I hope you see the objective, an aim in which I trust you all sympathize. Come, one and all, and praise the Lord. Is the invitation too wide? Observe the ninth verse: *"The Lord is good to all: and his tender mercies are over all his works. All thy works shall praise thee."* I will not limit the invitation of the Lord. Since you all drink of the river of His bounty, render to Him such praises as you can.

But there is a special invitation to His saints. Come and bless His name with spiritual, inward, enlightened praise. *"Bless the LORD, O house of Levi: ye that fear the LORD, bless the LORD"* (Psalm 135:20). In your heart of hearts extol, adore, and make Him great, for it is written, *"Thy saints shall bless thee"* (Psalm 145:10). Truly this was not written in vain. Let our souls bless the Lord today as the Holy Ghost moves within us.

We will focus on two things so that we may promote the objective we have in view.

The first is the method of securing the abundant utterance of God's praise as to His goodness; and the second, the motives for desiring to secure this abundant utterance.

To begin, let us discover the method of securing abundant utterance of divine praise concerning His goodness. Our text gives us the mental philosophy of abounding praise and shows us the plan by which such praise may be secured. The steps are such as the best philosophical logic approves.

First, we will be helped to abundant praise by **careful observation**. Notice the text: *"They shall abundantly utter the memory of thy great goodness."* In order to recall a memory, there must first of all be observation. A man does not remember what he never knew. This is clear to all, and therefore the point is virtually implied in the text. In proportion to the impression a fact or a truth makes on the mind, in that same proportion it is likely to abide in the memory. If you hear a sermon, that which you remember afterwards is the point which most forcibly strikes you while you are listening to the discourse. At the time, you say, "I will jot that down. I do not want to forget it, because it comes so closely home to me." Whether you use your pencil or not, memory obeys your wish and records it on her tablets.

The dealings of God towards us are just the same. If we want to remember His goodness, we must let it make an impression on us.

We must notice it, consider it, meditate on it, estimate it, and allow it to exert its due influence upon our hearts. Then we will not need to say that we must try to remember, for we will remember as a matter of course. The impression, having been clearly and deeply made, will not easily fade away, but we will recall it later. The first thing, therefore, towards the plentiful praising of God is a careful observation of His goodness.

Now, see what it is that we are to observe: God's goodness. Too many are blind to that **blessed object of observation**. They receive the bounties of providence, but do not see the hand of God in them. They are fed by His liberality and guided by His care, but attribute all that they receive to themselves or to secondary agents. God is not in all their thoughts, and consequently His goodness is not considered. They have no memory of His goodness because they have made no observation of it.

Some indeed, instead of observing the goodness of God, complain of His unkindness to them and imagine that He is needlessly severe. Like the unprofitable servant in the parable, they say, *"I knew thee, that thou art an hard man"* (Matthew 25:24). Others sit in judgment of His ways, as recorded in Holy Scripture, and dare to condemn the Judge of all the earth. Denying the goodness of Jehovah, they attempt to set up another God than the God of Abraham, Isaac, and Jacob, who for this enlightened century is a God much too sternly just. However, we worship Jehovah, the God of Abraham, Isaac, and Jacob, the Father of our Lord and Savior Jesus Christ, and none other than He. At present many adore new gods, unknown to our forefathers, not like the God of the Old Testament who in the opinion of modern philosophers is as much out of date as Jupiter himself. This day we say with David, *"This God is our God forever and ever"* (Psalm 48:14). *"O come, let us worship and bow down; let us kneel before the LORD our maker. For he is our God, and we are the people of his pasture, and the sheep of his hand"* (Psalm 95:6-7).

As we find the Lord revealed both in the Old and the New Testaments, making no division in the revelation, but regarding it as one grand whole, we behold abundant goodness in Him. Mingled with that awful justice which we would not wish to deny, we see surpassing grace, and we delight that God is love. He is gracious and full of compassion, slow to anger, and of great mercy. We have no complaints to make against Him. We wish to make no alteration in His dealings or in His character. He is our exceeding joy. The whole heart rejoices in the contemplation of Him. *"Who is like unto thee, O LORD? Among the gods who is like unto thee?"* (Exodus 15:11).

We are then to consider what many will not try to believe: that there is great goodness in Jehovah, the God of creation, providence, and redemption; the God of paradise, Sinai, and Calvary. We are to acquaint ourselves thoroughly with Him as He has made Himself known. We are continually to consider His great goodness, so that we may retain the memory of it.

If we are willing to see, we will not lack for **opportunities of beholding His goodness** every day. It is to be seen in so many acts that I will not begin the list, since I would never complete it. His goodness is seen in creation. It shines in every sunbeam, glitters in every dewdrop, smiles in every flower, and whispers in every breeze. Earth and sea and air, teeming with innumerable forms of life, are all full of the goodness of the Lord. Sun, moon, and stars affirm that the Lord is good, and all terrestrial things echo the proclamation. His goodness is also to be seen in the providence which rules over all. Let rebellious spirits murmur as they may, goodness is enthroned in God's kingdom, and evil and suffering are intruders there. God is good toward all His creatures, but especially toward the objects of His eternal love for whom all things work together for good.

However, we can see the noblest form of divine goodness in the domain of grace. Begin with the goodness which shines in our election. Follow the silver thread through redemption, the mission of the Holy Spirit, the calling, the adoption, the preservation, and the perfecting of the chosen. Then you will see riches of goodness which will astound you. Dwell where you may within the kingdom of redemption, and you will see rivers, even oceans of goodness. I leave it to your minds to remember these things and to your lips to speak abundantly of the memory of the Lord's great goodness in the wonders of His salvation. It is not my design to speak for you, but to stir you up to speak for yourselves.

The point which struck the psalmist, and should strike us all, **is the greatness of His goodness**. The greatness of the goodness will be seen by the contemplative mind by considering the person upon whom the goodness rests. "Why is this done to me?" will often be the utterance of a grateful spirit. That God should be good to any of His people shows His mercy, but that He should make me to be one of His and deal so well with me, here His goodness does exceed itself! *"Who am I, O LORD God, and what is my house?...Is this the manner of man, O LORD?* (2 Samuel 7:18, 19). It is great goodness, since it visits persons so insignificant, so guilty, and so deserving of wrath. Blessed be God that He is good to persons so ungrateful, to persons who cannot even at the best make any adequate return, who, alas, do not even make such return as they could. Lord, when I consider what a brutish creature I am, it is easy to confess the greatness of Your goodness.

The greatness of His goodness becomes apparent when we think **of the greatness of God the benefactor**. *"What is man that thou art mindful of him, or the son of man that thou visitest him?"* (Psalm 8:4). That God Himself should bless His people, that He should come in the form of human flesh to save His people, that He should dwell in us, walk with us, and be to us a God, a very present help in trouble, is a miracle of love. Is not this great goodness? I could very well understand the infinity of His benevolence commiting us to the charge of angels, but it is amazing that it is written, *"I the LORD do keep it: I will water it every moment: lest any hurt it, I will keep it night and day"* (Isaiah 27:3). Oh, the greatness of such personal condescension, such personal care! Heir of heaven, from the fountain of all goodness you will drink, and not from its streams alone. God Himself is your portion and the lot of your inheritance. You are not set aside with lesser creatures; the Creator Himself is yours. Will you not remember this, and so keep alive the memory of His goodness?

The greatness of the goodness is on some occasions made **manifest by the evil from which it rescues us**. Nobody knows the blessing of health as well as he who has been tortured with pain in every limb. Then he blesses Jehovah Rapha, the healing Lord, for his restoration. None know what salvation means like those who have been crushed under

15

the burden of guilt and have been racked by remorse. Did you ever feel yourself condemned by God and cast out from His presence? Did the pangs of hell commence in your startled conscience? Did your soul long for death rather than life, while thick clouds and darkness enshrouded your guilty spirit? If so, when the Lord has put away your sin and said, *"Thou shalt not die"* (2 Samuel 12:13), when He has brought you forth from prison, broken your chains, and set your feet upon a rock, then has the new song been in your mouth, even eternal praise. Then have you known it to be great goodness which thus delivered you.

We may imagine what the bottom of the sea is like, and conceive what it must be to be borne down to the lowest depths where seaweed is wrapped about dead men's brows. Yet, I assure you, our imaginations but poorly realize what Jonah experienced when the floods encompassed him and he sank to the bottom of the sea. When the Lord brought up his life from corruption, then he had a strong, vivid memory of the great goodness of God, knowing he had been delivered from such death.

It is in the storm that we learn to *"praise the LORD for His goodness, and for His wonderful works to the children of men"* (Psalm 107:8). If I might have it so, I could wish my whole life to be as calm as a fair summer's evening when scarcely a breeze stirs the happy flowers. I could desire that nothing might again disturb the serenity of my restful spirit. But were it to be so, I suspect I would know but little of the great goodness of the Lord. The sweet singer in Psalm 107 ascribes the song of gratitude not to dwellers at home, but to wanderers in the wilderness; not to those who are always at liberty, but to emancipated captives; not to the strong and vigorous, but to those who barely escape the gates of death; not to those who stand on a glassy sea, but to those who are tossed on a raging ocean.

Doubtless it is that we would not perceive the greatness of goodness if we did not see the depth of the horrible pit from which it snatches us. You were almost ruined in business, friend, but you escaped by the skin of your teeth. Then you praised God for His great goodness. The physicians gave up on your dear child, and your wife apparently sickened to the point of death, but both of these have been spared. Here you see the heights and depths of mercy. Now, therefore, lay up this great goodness in your memory to be the material for future psalms of praise.

Nor is this the only way of estimating God's great goodness. You may estimate it by the actual **greatness of the benefits bestowed**. He gives like a king—no, He gives as only God can give. Behold, your God has not given you a few minted coins of gold, but He has endowed you with the mines themselves. He has not, as it were, handed you a cup of cold water, but He has brought you to the flowing fountain and given the well itself to you. God Himself is ours: *"The LORD is my portion, saith my soul"* (Lamentations 3:24).

If you must have a little list of what He has given you, ponder the following: He has given you a name and a place among His people. He has given you the rights and the nature of His sons. He has given you the complete forgiveness of all your sins, and you have it now. He has given you a robe of righteousness which you are wearing now. He has given you a superlative loveliness in Christ Jesus. He has given you access to Him and acceptance at the mercy seat. He has given you this world and worlds to come. He has given you all that He has. He has given you His own Son, and how shall He now refuse you anything? Oh, He has given as only God could.

The greatness of His goodness this tongue can never hope to tell. As for myself, I will speak of my Lord as I find Him, for the old proverb bids us do so. Whatever you say, I have nothing to speak but what is good of my God, my King, from my childhood until now. He amazes me with His mercy. He utterly astounds me with His loving-kindness. He causes my spirit almost to swoon away with delight beneath the sweetness of His love.

Yet He has not spared me the rod, nor will He. Blessed be His name for that also. *"Shall we receive good at the hand of the God, and shall we not also receive evil?*" (Job 2:10) said the patriarch. But we will go beyond that and assert that evil is no evil when it comes from His hand. Everything is good which He ordains. We may not see it to be so at the time, but so it is. Our heavenly Father seems to rise from good to better, and from better to yet better still in infinite progression. He causes the roadways of our lives to rise higher and higher, and carries them over lofty mountains of loving-kindness. Our paths wind ever upward to yet higher summits of abounding mercy. Therefore, let His praise increase, and the name of the Lord be greater still.

I want to urge you, dear friends, to observe the goodness of God carefully for your souls' good. There is a great difference between eyes and no eyes. Yet, many have eyes and yet see not. God's goodness flows before them, but they say, "Where is it?" They breathe it but ask, "Where is it?" They sit at the table and are fed upon it. They wear it upon their limbs. It is in the very beating of their hearts, and yet they wonder, "Where is it?" Do not be so blind. *"The ox knoweth his owner, and the ass his master's crib"* (Isaiah 1:3). Let us not be slower than beasts of the field, but let us know the Lord and consider His great goodness.

I have said that the text contains the philosophy of great praise, and we see this in the second stage of the process, namely, diligent memory. That which has made an impression upon the mind by observation is fastened upon the memory. Memory seems to lie in two things: first, in retaining an impression, and then in recollecting it at a future time. I suppose that, more or less, everything that happens to us is retained in the mind, but it is not easy to reproduce the fainter impressions when you wish to do so. I know in my own mind a great many things that I am sure I remember, but yet I cannot always recall them instantly. Give me a quarter of an hour to run through a certain arrangement of ideas, and I can say, "Oh, yes, I have it. It was in my mind, but I could not recollect it at the time." Memory collects facts and afterwards recollects them. The matters before us are recorded by memory, but the tablet may be mislaid. The perfection of memory is to preserve the tablet in a well-known place from which you can bring it forth at any moment.

I have dwelt at length on observation with the idea that you may begin correctly from the very outset. By getting vivid impressions, you may be the better able to retain and to recall them. We cannot utter what we have forgotten. Thus, we need close observation to establish a strong memory concerning the Lord's great goodness.

How are we to strengthen our memory about God's goodness? First, we should **be well acquainted with the documents** in which His goodness is recorded. A man may be said to keep in memory a fact which did not happen in his own time, but hundreds of years before he was born. He remembers it because he has seen the document in which the fact is recorded. In a certain sense this is within the range of memory. It is within the memory of man, the united memory of the race, because it has been recorded and can be retrieved. Beloved, be familiar with the Word of God. Stock your memory with the ancient records of His great goodness. Drink in the whole narrative of the evangelists, and despise not Moses and the prophets. Soak in the Psalms, the Song of Solomon, and other such books until you come to know the well-recorded goodness of the Lord. Have His words and deeds of goodness arranged and ready at hand. Let them be at your finger tips, as it were, because they are in your heart's core. Then you will be sure abundantly to utter the memory of His goodness, for *"out of the abundance of the heart the mouth speaketh"* (Matthew 12:34).

Next, if you would strengthen your memory, **diligently observe memorials**. There are two in the Christian church. There is the memorial of your Savior's death, burial, and resurrection as set forth in believers' baptism, in which we are buried and risen with the Lord Christ. Forget not that memorial of His deep anguish when He was immersed in grief and plunged in agony, for He bids you observe it. As for the Holy Supper, never neglect it, but be

21

often at the table, where again you set forth His death until He come. He has bidden you to do this in remembrance of Him. Cherish devoutly the precious memorial. Great events in nations have been preserved in the memory of future generations by some ordained ceremonial. The Lord's Supper is of that kind. Therefore observe well the table of the Lord so that you forget not His great goodness. See how the Jews kept their Exodus in mind by means of the Paschal lamb; how they ate it after the sprinkling of the blood; how they talked to their children and told them of the deliverance from Egypt, abundantly uttering the memory of God's goodness; and how after supper they sang a hymn, even as our text bids us to sing of the goodness of God. Strengthen your memories, then, by reverent attention to the historical documents and the memorial ordinances.

Still, the most important is the memory of what has happened to yourself, your own **personal experience**. I will not give a penny for your religion unless it has taken effect on you. The power of prayer! What of that? Did you ever receive an answer to prayer? Did you ever wrestle with the angel and come away victorious? What do you know about prayer if you never did? You are very orthodox, but unless the doctrines of grace have brought to your soul the grace of the doctrines, and you have tasted and handled them, what do you know about them? You have nothing to remember.

O, dear heart, were you ever born again? Then you will remember His great goodness. Were you ever cleansed from your sin and justified in Christ? You will remember His great goodness. Have you been renewed in heart so as to hate sin and live in holiness? If so, you will remember, because you know something which flesh and blood has not revealed unto you. Let every personal mercy be written upon your personal memory.

I have heard that the practice of mnemonics, or the strengthening of the memory—for which I do not have a very high esteem—lies in the following of certain methods. According to some, you **link one idea with another** and recollect a date by associating it with something that you can see. Practice this method in the present case. Remember God's goodness by the objects around you which are associated with it. For instance, let your bed remind you of God's mercy in the night watches, and let your table bring to remembrance His goodness in supplying your daily needs. My garments, when I put them on this morning, reminded me of times when my hand was not capable even of that simple task. All around us there are memoranda of God's love if we choose to read them. The memory of some deed of divine goodness may be connected with every piece of furniture in your room. There is the old armchair where you wrestled with God in great trouble and received a gracious answer. You cannot forget it. You do not pray as well anywhere else as you do there. You have become attached to that particular chair. That well-thumbed Bible—your special one—is getting rather worn now and is marked up a good deal. Nevertheless, out of that very copy the promises have gleamed forth like the stars in heaven, and so it helps your memory to use it.

I remember a poor man giving me what I thought great praise. I visited him in the hospital, and he said, "You seem to have filled this room with your texts, for everything reminds me of what I have heard you say. As I lie here, I recall your stories and sayings." In much the same way, we should recollect what God has done for us by looking at the various places, circumstances, times, and persons which were the surroundings of His mercy. O for a clear remembrance of God's goodness.

Memory is sometimes helped by **classification**. When you send your maid to a shop for a variety of articles, she may forget something unless you arrange the order of the list so that one suggests another. Take care to set God's mercies in order. Enumerate them as you can, and so fix them in your memory.

At other times, when persons have very bad memories, they like to jot down on a bit of paper that which is important to remember. I have often done so, and then have placed the paper where I have never found it again. A thread tied around the finger and many other

memory devices have been tried. I do not mind what it is, so long as you try to recall God's mercy to you by some means or other. Do make some record of His goodness. You know the day in which you lost that money, do you not? "Yes, very well." You recall the day of the month of Black Friday, or Black Monday, up in the city. You have evil days indelibly noted in the black pocketbook of memory. Do you remember as well the days of God's special loving-kindness to you? You should do so. Carefully take note of noteworthy benefits and mark remarkable blessings. Thus, shall you in future days *"abundantly utter the memory of God's great goodness."*

The first two processes for securing abundant praise are observation and remembrance. The next is **utterance**: *"They shall abundantly utter."* The word contains the idea of boiling or bubbling up like a fountain. It signifies a holy fluency about the mercy of God. We have quite enough fluent people about, but many of them are idlers for whom Satan finds abundant things to say. It matters not how fluent men and women are, if they will be fluent on the topic now before us. Open your mouths. Let the praise pour forth. Let it come, rivers of it. Stream away! Gush away, all that you possibly can. *"They shall abundantly utter the memory of thy great goodness."* Do not stop the joyful speakers. Let them go on forever. They do not exaggerate, for they cannot. You say they are enthusiastic, but they are not half up to pitch yet. Encourage them to become more excited and speak even more fervently. Go on, go on. Pile it up. Say something greater, grander, and more fiery still! You cannot exceed the truth. You have come to a theme where your most fluent powers will fail in utterance. The text calls for a sacred fluency, and I would exhort you liberally to exercise it when you are speaking of the goodness of God.

"They shall abundantly utter [it]." That is, they will constantly be doing it. They will talk about God's goodness all day long. When you step into their cottages, they will begin to tell you of God's goodness to them. When you bid adieu to them at night, you will hear more last words upon the favorite theme. Very likely they will repeat themselves, but that does not matter. You cannot have too much of this truly good thing. Just as the singers in the temple repeated again and again the chorus, *"His mercy endureth forever,"* so may we repeat our praises. Some of God's mercies are so great and sweet that, if we never had another throughout eternity, the recollection of the single favor might forever remain. The splendor of divine love is so great that a single manifestation of it is often all that we can bear. To have two such revelations at once would be as overpowering as if God would make two suns when one already fills the world with light. Oh, praise the Lord with boundless exultation. Rouse all your

faculties to this service, and *"abundantly utter the memory of [his] great goodness."*

You cannot praise abundantly unless your memory supplies materials. On the other hand your memory will lose strength unless you utter what you know. When you went to school and had a lesson to learn, you found out that, by reading your lesson aloud, you learned it more quickly because your ear assisted your eye. Uttering the divine goodness is a great help to the memory of it. By teaching, we learn. By giving the truth expression, we deepen its impression upon our minds.

Now I come to the last part of this admirable process. When we have abundantly uttered, then we are to **sing**. In the old Greek mythology Mnemosynè, the goddess of memory, is the mother of the Muses, and surely where there is a good memory of God's lovingkindness, the heart will soon produce a song. But what is surprising in the text is that when the joy is described as mounting from simple utterance to song it takes on another theme: *"...sing of thy righteousness."* When the heart is most adoring and selects the grandest theme for reverent song, it chooses the meeting of goodness and righteousness as its topic. How sweet is that melody:

> "Mercy and truth are met together,
> And righteousness and peace
> Have kissed each other."

The atonement is the gem of the heart's poetry. Do not your hearts burn within you at the very mention of the glorious deed of Jesus our great Substitute? Parnassus is outdone by Calvary; the Castalian spring is dried up and Jesus' wounded side has opened another fountain of song. The goodness of the Lord to us in all the blessings of His providence we gladly recite, but when we tell of the grace which led our Lord Jesus Christ to bleed and die, *"the just for the unjust, that he might bring us to God"* (1 Peter 3:18), our music leaps to nobler heights. Incomparable wisdom ordained a way in which God could be righteous to the sternness of severity, and yet could be good, illimitably good, to those that put their trust in Him. Lift up then your music until the golden harps find themselves outdone.

Thus, we have explained the method of securing an abundant utterance. May the Holy Spirit help us to carry it out.

Now, we will very briefly note **the motives for this abundant utterance**. These lie very near at hand. The first is, because we cannot help it. The goodness of God demands that we should speak of it. If the Lord Jesus Himself would charge His people to be silent as to His goodness, they would scarcely be able to obey the command. They would, like the man that was healed, blaze abroad the mighty work that He had done. But, bless His name, He has not told us to be quiet. He allows us to utter the memory of His great goodness abundantly. The stones of the street would cry out as we went along if we did not speak of His love.

Some of you good people seldom speak of the goodness of God. Why is this? I wonder how you can be so coldly quiet. "Oh," said one in his first love, "I must speak or I shall burst." We have sometimes felt the same, when restrained testimony became fire within our bones. Is it not a sacred instinct to tell what we feel within? The news is too good to keep. Indulge to the full the holy propensity of your renewed nature. Your soul says, "Speak." If etiquette says, "Hush, they will think you a fanatic," regard it not, but speak aloud. Let them think you are a fanatic if they please. Play the organ softly when the subject is your own praise, but when it comes to the praises of God, pull out all the stops. Thunderous music is too little for His infinite deserving.

Another motive for abundantly uttering the praises of God is that other voices are clamorous to drown it. What a noisy world this is with its conflicting, discordant cries. "Here," cries one. "Look there," shouts another. This uproar would drown the notes of God's praise unless His people uttered it again and yet again. The more there is said against our God, the more should we speak for Him.

Whenever you hear a man curse, it would be wise to say aloud, "Bless the Lord." Say it seven times for every time he curses, and make him hear it. Perhaps he will want to know what you are doing, which will then give you an opportunity of asking what he is doing. He will have more difficulty in explaining himself than you will in explaining yourself. Do try if you can to make up for the injuries done to the dear and sacred name of God by multiplying your praises in proportion as you hear Him spoken ill of. I say, unless you give forth abundant utterance, God's praise will be buried under heaps of blasphemy, ribaldry, nonsense, error, and idle talk. Abundantly utter it so that some of it, at least, may be heard.

Praise the Lord abundantly because it will benefit you to do so. How bright the past looks when we begin to praise God for it. When we say, *"I am the man that hath seen affliction"* (Lamentations 3:1), we are to fill the cup of memory with gall and wormwood. But when we see the goodness of God in it all, we turn the kerchief with which we wiped our tears into a flag of victory, and with holy praise, in the name of our God, we wave His banner.

As for the present, if you think of God's mercies, how different it seems. A man comes to his dinner table and does not enjoy what is there, because he misses an expected dainty. But if he were as poor as some people, he would not turn his nose up, but would bless the goodness which has given him so much more than he deserves. Some people I know even among Christians are growlers, in general always finding fault. The best things in the world are not good enough for them. Oh, beloved, *"abundantly utter the memory of God's great goodness,"* and you will find nothing to grumble at, nothing to complain about, but everything to rejoice in.

As for the future, if we remember God's goodness, how joyfully we will march into it. There is the same goodness for tomorrow as for yesterday, and the same goodness for old age as for youth; the same God to bless me when I grow gray as when I was a babe at my mother's breast. Therefore, I go forward to the future without hesitation or suspicion, abundantly recounting the loving-kindness of the Lord.

Again, I think we ought to do this because of the good it does for other people. If you abundantly talk of God's goodness, you are sure to benefit your neighbors. Many are comforted when they hear of God's goodness to their friends. Draw a long face and lament the trials of the way. Sit down with somber brethren and enjoy a little comfortable misery. Then see whether crowds will ask to share your vinegar cruet.

"While here our various wants we mourn,
    United groans ascend on high,"

says Dr. Watts, and I am afraid he speaks the truth. However, very few will be led in this way to resolve, *"We will go with you, for we have heard that God is with you"* (Zechariah 8:23). Is it good reasoning if men say, "These people are so miserable that they must be on the way to heaven"? We may hope they are, for they evidently want some better place to live in. But then it may be questioned if such folks would not be wretched even in heaven. Dear friends, you would not be much attracted by sanctimonious misery. Therefore, do not try it yourselves.

On the contrary, talk much of the goodness of the Lord, wear a smiling face, let your eyes sparkle, and go through the world as if, after all, you are not slaves under the lash, or prisoners in bonds, but the Lord's free men. We have glorious reasons for being happy. Let us be so, and soon we will hear people asking, "What is this? Is this religion? I thought religious people felt bound to be down in the dumps, and to go mourning and sighing all their days." When they see your joy, they will be tempted to come to Christ. There is a blessed seductiveness in a holy, happy life. Praise His name for evermore. *"Abundantly utter the memory of his great goodness,"* and you will bring many to Christ.

Such happy utterance will help also to comfort your own Christian friends and fellow-sufferers. There is a deal of misery in the world—now more than usual. Many are sorrowing from various causes. Therefore, my dear friends, be happier than ever before. That venerable man of God, now in heaven, our dear old Dransfield, when it was a very foggy morning in November, used always to come into the vestry before the sermon and say, "It is a dreary morning, dear pastor. We must rejoice in the Lord more than usual. Things around us are dark, but within and above all is bright. I hope we shall have a very happy service today." He would shake hands with me and smile, until he seemed to carry us all into the middle of summer. What if it is bad weather? Bless the Lord that it is not worse than it is. We are not altogether in Egyptian darkness. The sun does shine now and then, and we are sure it has not blown out. So, when we are sick and ill, let us thank God that we shall not be ill forever, for there is a place where the inhabitants are never sick. Today, if your harps have been hanging on the willows, take them down; if you have not praised the Lord as you should, begin to do so. Wash your mouths and get rid of the sour flavor of murmuring about bad trade and bad weather.

Sweeten your lips with the pleasant confection of praise. If anyone should confess to me that he has sinned by going too far in blessing God, I would for once become a priest and give him absolution. I never tried my hand at that business before, but I think I can manage that much. Praise God extravagantly if you can. Try it. Say to yourself, "I will go beyond all boundaries in this matter," for there are no limits to the deserving of God who ever blesses.

Lastly, let us praise and bless God because it is the way in which He is glorified. We cannot add to His glory, for it is infinite in itself, but we can make it more widely known by simply stating the truth about Him. Do you not want to give honor to God? Would you not lay down your life that the whole earth might be filled with His glory? Well, if you cannot cover the earth with His praise as the waters cover the sea, you can at least contribute your portion to the flood.

Do not keep back your praises, but bless and magnify His name, *"from the rising of the sun to the going down of the same"* (Psalm 113:3). It will lift earth upward and heavenward if we all unite in praise. We will see it rising as it were beneath our feet, and ourselves rising with it, until we stand as upon the top of some lofty alp that has pierced the vault of heaven. We will be among the angels, feeling as they feel, doing as they do, and losing ourselves as they lose themselves in the eternal hallelujah of *"Blessing, and honor, and glory, and power be unto him that sitteth upon the throne, and unto the Lamb for ever and ever"* (Revelation 5:13).

Chapter 2

More and More

*"But I will hope continually, and will yet praise
thee more and more."*
—Psalm 71:14

When sin conquered the realm of manhood,
it slew all the minstrels except those of
hope. For humanity, amid all its sorrows and
sins, hope sings on. To believers in Jesus there
remains a royal race of minstrels, for we have a
hope of glory, a lively hope, a hope eternal and
divine. Because our hope abides, our praise
continues. *"I will hope continually, and will yet
praise thee."* Because our hopes grow brighter
and are every day nearer and nearer to their
fulfillment, the volume of our praise increases.
*"I will hope continually, and will yet praise
thee more and more."*

A dying hope would bring forth declining
songs. As the expectations grow more dim, so
would the music become more faint. But a
hope immortal and eternal, flaming forth each

day with more intense brightness, brings forth a song of praise which always gathers new force as it continues to arise. See well to your faith and your hope, for otherwise God will be robbed of His praise. It will be in proportion as you hope for the good things which He has promised to your faith, that you will render to Him the praise which is His royal revenue, acceptable to Him by Jesus Christ, and abundantly due from you.

David had not been slack in praise. Indeed, he was a sweet singer in Israel, a very choir master unto the Lord. Yet he vowed to praise Him more and more. Those who do much already are usually the people who can do more. David was old. Would he praise God more when he was infirm than he had done when he was young and vigorous? If he could not excel with loudness of voice, yet would he with eagerness of heart. What his praise might lack in sound, it should gain in solemn earnestness. He was in trouble too, yet he would not allow the heyday of his prosperity to surpass in its notes of loving adoration the dark hour of his adversity. For him on no account could there be any going back.

David had adored the Lord when he was but a youth and kept his father's flock. Harp in hand, beneath the spreading tree, he had worshipped the Lord his Shepherd, whose rod and staff were his comfort and delight. When he was an exile, he had made the rocky fortresses of Adullam and Engedi resound with the name of Jehovah. Later, when he had become king in Israel, his psalms had been multiplied and his harp strings were daily accustomed to the praises of the God of his salvation.

How could that zealous songster make an advance in praise? See him dancing before the ark of the Lord with all his might; what more of joy and zeal can be manifest? Yet he says, *"I will yet praise thee more and more."* His troubles had been multiplied of late, and his infirmities too. Yet for all that, no murmuring escaped him, but he resolved that his praise would rise higher and higher until he continued it in better lands forever and ever.

Beloved, I pray that the Holy Spirit may make my word stimulating to you. Our subject is that of our praising God more and more. I do not intend to entreat you to praise God, but will take it for granted that you are doing so, though I fear it will be a great mistake in the case of many. Those who do not praise God at all cannot be urged to praise Him more and more. I am directing myself to those who now love to praise God. I charge you to resolve with David: *"I will yet praise thee more and more."*

Our first business will be to urge ourselves to this resolution. Why should we praise God more and more? I am overwhelmed with the multitude of arguments which beset me. So many crowd around me that I cannot number them in order, but must seize them at random.

It is humbling to remember that we may very well praise God more than we have done, for **we have praised Him very little as yet**. What we have done, as believers, in glorifying God falls far, far short of His due. Personally, upon consideration, we each must admit this. Think, my dear believer, what the Lord has done for you. Some years ago you were in sin, death, and ruin, but He called you by His grace. You were under the burden and curse of sin, but He delivered you. Did you not expect in your first joy of pardon to have done more for Him, to have loved Him more, to have served Him better? What are the returns which you have made for the blessings which you have received? Are they at all fitting or adequate? I look at a field loaded with precious grain and ripening for the harvest. I hear that the husbandman has expended so much in rent, so much on the plowing, so much in enriching the soil, so much for seed, so much more for necessary weeding. There is the harvest, which yields a profit: he is contented.

I see another field. It is my own heart, and yours is the same. What has the Husbandman done for it? He has reclaimed it from the wild waste by a power no less then omnipotent. He has hedged it, plowed it, and cut down the thorns. He has watered it as no other field was ever watered, for the bloody sweat of Christ has bedewed it, to remove the primeval curse. God's own Son has given His all so that this barren waste may become a garden. What has been done would be hard to enumerate. What more could have been done none can say. Yet what is the harvest? Is it adequate to the labor expended? Is the tillage remunerative? I am afraid if we cover our faces, or if a blush serves us instead of a veil, it will be the most fit reply to the question. Here and there a withered ear is a poor recompense for the tillage of infinite love. Let us, therefore, be shamed into a firm resolve and say with resolute spirit, "By the good help of infinite grace, I, at any rate, having been so great a laggard, will quicken my pace. *'I will yet praise thee more and more.'"*

Another argument which presses upon my mind is this: when we have praised God up until now, we have not found the service to be a weariness to ourselves, but it has ever been to us both **a profit and a delight**. I would not speak falsely even for God, but I bear my testimony that the happiest moments I have ever spent have been occupied with the worship of God. I have never been so near heaven as when adoring before the eternal throne. I think every Christian could say the same. Among all the joys of earth—and I will not depreciate them—there is no joy comparable to that of praise. The innocent mirth of the fireside, the chaste happiness of household love, even these are not to be mentioned side by side with the joy of worship, the rapture of drawing near to the Most High. Earth, at her best, yields but water, but this divine occupation is as the wine of Cana's marriage feast.

The purest and most exhilarating joy is the delight of glorifying God and anticipating the time when we will enjoy Him forever. Now, if God's praise has been no wilderness to you, return to it with zest and ardor, saying, *"I will yet praise thee more and more."* If any suppose that you grow weary with the service of the Lord, tell them that His praise is such freedom, such recreation, such felicity, that you desire never to cease from it. As for me, if men call God's service slavery, I desire to be a bondslave forever and would be branded with my Master's name indelibly. I would have my ear bored to the doorpost of my Lord's house, and go no more out. My soul joyfully sings:

> "Let thy grace, Lord, like a fetter,
> Bind my wandering heart to thee."

This will be my ambition—to be more and more subservient to the divine honor. This shall be gain—to be nothing for Christ's sake. This my all in all—to praise You, my Lord, as long as I have any being.

A third reason readily suggests itself. We ought surely to praise God more today than any other previous day **because we have received more mercies**. Even of temporal favors we have been large partakers. Begin with these, and then rise higher. Some of you may well be reminded of the great temporal mercies which have been lavished upon you. You are today in a similar state with Jacob when he said, *"With my staff I passed over this Jordan, and now I am become two bands"* (Genesis 32:10). When you first left your father's house to follow a toilsome occupation, you had a scant enough purse and but poor prospects, but where are you now as to temporal circumstances and position? How highly God has favored some of you! Joseph has risen from the dungeon to the throne; David has gone up from the sheepfold to a palace. Look back to what you were, and give the Lord His due. *"He raiseth the poor from the dust...to set them among princes"* (1 Samuel 2:8). You were unknown and insignificant, and now His mercy has placed you in prominence and esteem. Is this nothing? Do you despise the bounty of heaven? Will you not praise the Lord more and more for this? Surely, you should and must do so, or else feel the withering curse which blasts ingratitude wherever it dwells.

Perhaps divine providence has not dealt with you exactly in that way, but with equal goodness and wisdom has revealed itself to you in another form. You have continued in the same sphere in which you commenced, but you have been enabled to pursue your work, have been kept in health and strength, and have been supplied with food and clothing. Best of all, you have been blessed with a contented heart and a gleaming eye. My dear friend, are you not thankful? Will you not praise your heavenly Father more and more?

We ought not to overemphasize temporal mercies so as to become worldly, but I am afraid there is a greater likelihood of our understating them and becoming ungrateful. We must beware of so undervaluing them as to lessen our sense of the debt which we owe God.

We must speak of **great mercies** sometimes. Come now, I will ask you a question: Can you count your great mercies? I cannot count mine. Perhaps you think the enumeration is easy. I find it endless. I was thinking the other day what a great mercy it was to be able to turn over in bed. Some of you smile, perhaps. Yet I do not exaggerate when I say I clapped my hands for joy when I found myself able to turn in bed without pain. Right now, it is to me a very great mercy to be able to stand upright. We carelessly imagine that there are but a score or two of great mercies, such as having our children about us or enjoying good health. But in trying times we see that many minor matters are also great gifts of divine love and entail great misery when they are withdrawn. Sing, then, as you draw water at the springs. As the brimming vessels overflow, *"praise ye the Lord yet more and more."*

But ought we not to praise God more and more when we think of our spiritual mercies? What favors have we received of this higher sort! Ten years ago you were bound to praise God for the covenant mercies you had even then enjoyed. Now, how many more have been bestowed upon you? How many cheerings amid darkness? How many answers to prayer? How many directions in dilemma? How many delights of fellowship? How many helps in service? How many successes in conflict? How many revelations of infinite love? To adoption there has been added all the blessings of being an heir; to justification, all the security of acceptance; to conversion, all the energies of indwelling.

Remember, as there was no silver cup in Benjamin's sack until Joseph put it there, so there was no spiritual good in you until the Lord of mercy gave it. Therefore, praise the Lord. Louder and louder still may your song be. Praise Him on the high-sounding cymbals. Since we cannot hope to measure His mercies, let us immeasurably praise our God. *"I will yet praise thee more and more."*

Let us go on a little farther. All of us have **proved through the years the faithfulness, immutability, and veracity of God**: proving these attributes by their bearing the strain of our misbehavior when we sin against God; proving them by the innumerable benefits the Lord bestows on us. Will all this experience end in no result? Will there be no growth in gratitude where there is such an increase of obligation? God is so good that every moment of His love demands a lifetime of praise.

It should never be forgotten that every Christian, as he grows in grace, should have a **loftier idea of God**. Our highest conception of God falls infinitely short of His glory, but a mature Christian enjoys a far clearer view of what God is than he had at the first. Now, the **greatness of God** is ever a claim for praise. *"Great is the Lord, and"*—what follows?— *"greatly to be praised."* If God is greater to me than He was before, let my praise be greater. If I think of Him more tenderly as my Father, if I have a clearer view of Him in the terror of His justice, if I have a clearer view of the splendors of His wisdom by which He devised the atonement, if I have larger thoughts of His eternal, immutable love, let every advance in knowledge constrain me to say, *"I will yet praise thee more and more."*

May I sincerely pray, *"'I heard of thee by the hearing of the ear, but now mine eye seeth thee: wherefore* [while] *I abhor myself and repent in dust and ashes'* (Job 42:5-6), my praise for You will rise yet more loftily. Up to Your throne will my song ascend. I only saw the skirts of Your garment, as it were, but You have hidden me in the cleft of the rock, Jesus, and made Your glory pass before me. I will praise You even as the seraphim do, and compete with those before the throne in magnifying Your name." We learn but little in Christ's school, if the practical result of it all does not make us cry, *"I will yet praise thee more and more."*

Still culling here and there a thought out of thousands, I would remind you that it is a good reason for praising God more that we are **getting nearer to the place, world without end, where we hope to praise Him perfectly**. Never do the church walls ring more joyously than when the congregation unites in singing about the Father's house on high and having tents pitched, "A day's march nearer home."

Heaven is indeed the only home of our souls, and we will never feel that we have come to our rest until we have reached its mansions. One reason why we will be able to rest in heaven is because there we will be able perpetually to achieve the object of our creation. Am I nearer heaven? Then I will be doing more of the work which I will do in heaven. I will soon use the harp, so let me be carefully tuning it. Let me rehearse the hymns which I will sing before the throne. Even though the words in heaven will be sweeter and richer than any that poets can assemble together here, yet the essential song of heaven will be the same as that which we are presenting to Jehovah here below:

> "They praise the Lamb in hymns above,
>   And we in hymns below."

The essence of their praise is gratitude that He suffered and shed His blood; it is the essence of our praise, too. They bless Immanuel's name for undeserved favors bestowed upon unworthy ones, and we do the same.

My aged brothers and sisters, I congratulate you, for you are almost home. Be yet more full of praise than ever. Quicken your footsteps as the glorious land shines more brightly. You are close to the pearly gates. Sing on, though your infirmities increase. Let the song grow sweeter and louder until it melts into the infinite harmonies.

Do I need to give another reason why we should praise God more and more? If I must, I would throw this one into the scale, that surely at this present juncture we ought to be more earnest in the praise of God **because God's enemies are very earnest in laboring to dishonor Him**. These are times when scoffers are boundlessly impudent. Do you not become angered when you read of French revolutionists talk of having "demolished God"? It strikes me as even a sadder thing when I read the propositions of their philosophies that suggest they should become religious again and should bring God back for another ten years at least—an audacious recommendation as blasphemously impertinent as the insolence which had proclaimed the triumph of atheism.

Perhaps, however, the Parisians speak more honestly than we do here, for among us we have abounding infidelity which pretends to reverence Scripture while it denies its clearest teachings. Also we have what is quite as bad, a superstition which thrusts Christ aside for the human priest, elevates the sacraments as everything, and makes simple trust in the great atonement to be as nothing. Now, those who hold these views are not sleepers, nor do they relax their efforts. Alas, we may be very quiet and lukewarm about religion, but these persons are earnest propagators of their faith, or no faith—they will cover sea and land to make one proselyte. As we think of these busy servants of Satan, we ought to chide ourselves and say, "Shall Baal be so diligently served, and Jehovah have such a sleepy advocate? Be stirred, my soul! Awake, my spirit! Rise up at once, and praise your God more and more."

But, indeed, while I give you these few arguments out of many that come to mind, the thought cheers my spirit that with those of you who know and love God, there is little need for me to mention reasons **because your own souls hunger and thirst to praise Him**. If you are stopped for a little time from the public service of God, you pant for the assemblies of God's house and envy the swallows that build their nests beneath the eaves. If you are unable to accomplish the service which you were accustomed to performing for Christ's church, the hours drag wearily along. As the Master found it His meat and His drink to do the will of Him that sent Him, so also when you are unable to do that will, you too are like a person deprived of his meat and drink, and an insatiable hunger grows in you. Christian, do you yearn to praise God? I am sure you feel now, "O that I could praise Him better!"

You are perhaps in a position in which you have work to do for Him, and your heart is saying, "How I wish I could do this work more thoroughly to His praise!" Or possibly you are in such a condition of life that it is little you can do, and you often wish if God would make a change for you, not that it should be one more full of comfort, but one in which you could be more serviceable. Above all, I know you wish you were rid of sin and everything which hinders your praising God more and more. Well, then, I need not argue, for your own heart pleads the holy cause.

Allow me to illustrate this point with a story. I know a person who has been long privileged to lift his voice in the choir of the great King. In that delightful labor none was more happy than he. The longer he was engaged in the work the more he loved it. Now, it came to pass that on a certain day, this songster found himself shut out of the choir. He would have entered to take his part, but he was not permitted. Perhaps the King was angry; perhaps the songster had sung carelessly; perhaps he had acted unworthily in some other matter; or possibly His master knew that his song would grow sweeter if he were silenced for awhile. How it was I know not, but this I know, that it caused great searching of heart. Often this chorister begged to be restored, but he was just as often repulsed, and somewhat roughly, too. For more than three months that this unhappy songster was kept in enforced silence, with fire in his bones and no vent for it. The royal music went on without him. There was no lack of song, for which he rejoiced, but he longed to take his place again. I cannot tell you how eagerly he longed. At last the happy hour arrived. The King gave his permission that he might sing again. The songster was full of gratitude, and I heard him say, "My Lord, since I am again restored, *'I will hope continually, and will yet praise thee more and more.'* "

Now let us turn to another point. Let us in the Spirit's strength drive away all **hinderances to praising God** more and more.

One of the deadliest things is **dreaminess or sleepiness**. A Christian readily falls into this state. I notice it even in the public congregation. Very often the whole service is gone through mechanically. That same dreaminess falls on many who profess and abides with them. Instead of praising God more and more, it is every bit as hard for them to keep up the old strain—and just barely so. Let us shake ourselves from all such lethargy. Surely if there were any service in which a man would be wholly awake and alert, it is in praising and magnifying God. A sleepy angel at the throne of God or a cherub nodding during sacred song is ridiculous to imagine. Will such an insult to the majesty of heaven be seen on earth? No! Let us say to all that is within us, "Awake!"

The next hindrance would be **a divided focus**. We cannot, however we may resolve, praise God more and more if, as we grow older, we allow this world to take up our thoughts. If I say, *"I will yet praise thee more and more,"* and yet I am striking out right and left with projects of amassing wealth, or I am plunging myself into greater business cares unnecessarily, my actions belie my resolutions. Not that we would check enterprise. There are periods in life when a man may be enabled to praise God more and more by extending the bounds of his business. But there are persons whom I have known who have praised God very well in a certain condition, but they have not been content to let well enough alone and have been set on aggrandizing themselves. They have had to give up teaching Sunday school, attendance with the visitation committee, or some other form of Christian service because their money-getting demanded all their strength. Beloved, you shall find it small gain if you gain in this world, but lose in praising God. As we grow older, it is wise to concentrate more and more of our energies upon the one thing, the only thing worth living for—the praise of God.

Another great obstacle to praising God more is **self-contentment**. This, again, is a condition into which we may very easily fall. Our real belief is—only we never say it when we may be overheard—that we are all very fine fellows indeed. We may confess when we are praying, as well as at other times, that we are miserable sinners, and I dare say we have some belief that it is so. But for all that, there is within our minds the conviction that we are very respectable people and are doing exceedingly well on the whole. Comparing ourselves with other Christians, it is much to our credit that we are praising God as well as we are. Now, I have put this very roughly, but is it not what the heart has said to us at times? Such a loathsome thought it is that a sinner should grow content with himself.

Self-satisfaction is the end of progress. Dear friend, why compare yourself with the dwarfs around you? If you must compare yourself with others, look at the giants of former days. Better still, relinquish altogether the evil habit, for Paul tells us it is not wise to compare ourselves among ourselves. (See 2 Corinthians 10:12-14.) Look to our Lord and Master, who towers so high above us in peerless excellence. No, we dare not flatter ourselves, but with humble self-abasement we resolve to praise the Lord more and more.

To rest on past laurels is another danger. We did so much for God when we were young. Occasionally I have met with drones in the Christian hive whose boast is that they made a great deal of honey years ago. I see men resting on their oars today, but they startle me with a description of the impetus they gave to the boat years ago. You should have seen them in those former times, when they were master-rowers. What a pity that these brothers cannot be aroused to do their first works. It would be a gain to the church, but it would be an equal benefit to themselves. Suppose God would say, "Rest on the past. I gave you great mercies twenty years ago; live on them." Suppose the eternal and ever-beloved Spirit would say, "I did a great work in you thirty years ago. I withdraw Myself, and I will do no more." Where would you be then? Yes, if you still have to draw afresh upon the eternal fountains, do praise the Source of all.

May God help us then to shake off all those things which would prevent our praising Him! Possibly there is some afflicted one, in so low a state, so far pressed by poverty or bodily pain, that he is saying, "I cannot praise God more and more. I am ready to despair." Dear believer, may God give you **full submission to His will**. Then the greater your troubles, the sweeter will be your song.

I heard from an old parson a short, sweet story which touched my heart. A poor widow and her little child were sitting together in great want, both feeling the pinch of hunger.

The child looked up into the mother's face, and said, "Mother, God won't starve us, will He?" "No, my child," said the mother, "I do not think He will." "But, mother," said the child, "if He does, we will still praise Him as long as we live, won't we, mother?" May those who are gray-headed be able to say what the child said, and to carry it out. *"Though he slay me, yet will I trust in him"* (Job 13:15). *"Shall we receive good at the hands of God, and shall we not receive evil?"* (Job 2:10). *"The LORD gave, and the LORD hath taken away; blessed be the name of the LORD."* (Job 1:21). *"I will yet praise thee more and more."*

Very briefly, let us apply ourselves to the **practical carrying out of this resolution**. I have given you arguments for it and tried to move away impediments. Now for a little help in the performance of it. How do we begin to praise God more and more?

Earnestness says, "I will undertake some fresh duty this afternoon." Stop just a minute. If you want to praise God, would not it be as well first to begin with yourself? The musician said, "I will praise God better," but the pipes of his instrument were foul. He had better look to them first. If the strings have slipped from their proper tension, it would be well to correct them before beginning the tune. If we would praise God more, it is not to be done as boys rush into a bath—head first. No, prepare yourself by **making your heart ready**. You need the Spirit's aid to make your soul fit for praising God. It is not every fool's work. Go then to your chamber, confess the sins of the past, and ask the Lord to give you much more grace that you may begin to praise Him.

If we would praise God more and more, let us **improve our private devotions**. God is much praised by really devout prayer and adoration. Preaching is not fruit: it is sowing. True song is fruit. I mean this: that the green blade of the wheat may be the sermon, but the kernel of wheat is the hymn you sing, the prayer in which you unite. The true result of life is praise to God. "The chief end of man," says the catechism, and I cannot put it better, "is to glorify God, and enjoy Him forever." When we glorify God in our private devotions, we are answering the true end of our being. If we desire to praise God more, we must ask for grace that our private devotions may rise to a higher standard. I am more and more persuaded from my own experience that, in proportion to the strength of our private lives with God, so will be the force of our character and the power of our work for Him among men. Let us look well to this.

Again, however, I hear the zealous young man or woman saying, "Well, I will attend to what you have said. I will see to private prayer and to heart work, but I mean to begin some work of usefulness." Quite right, but wait a little. I want to ask you this question: Are you sure that your own **personal conduct in your everyday life** has as much of the praise of God in it as it might have? It is all a mistake to think that we must come to a church building to praise God. You can praise God in your shops, in your kitchens, and in your bedrooms. It is all a mistake to suppose that Sunday is the only day to praise God in. Praise Him on Mondays, Tuesdays, Wednesdays, every day, everywhere. All places are holy to holy people, and all engagements holy to holy men, if they do them with holy motives, lifting up their hearts to God. Whether a man swings the blacksmith's hammer or lays his hand to the plow, that which is done as unto the Lord and not unto men is true worship.

I like the story of the maidservant, who, when she was asked on joining the church, "Are you converted?" "I hope so, sir." "What makes you think you are really a child of God?" "Well, sir, there is a great change in me from what there used to be." "What is that change?" "I don't know, sir, but there is a change in all things. But there is one thing, I always sweep under the mats now." Many a time she had hidden the dust under the mat. It was not so now. It is a very excellent reason for believing that there is a change of heart when work is conscientiously done.

There is a set of mats in all our houses where we are accustomed to hiding the dirt away. When a man in his business sweeps from under the mats—you merchants have your mats, you know—when he avoid the evils which custom tolerates but which God condemns, then he has marks of grace within. Oh, to have a conduct molded by the example of Christ! If any man lived a holy life, though he never preached a sermon or even sang a hymn, he would have praised God. The more conscientiously he acted, the more thoroughly would he have done so.

These inner matters being considered, let us go on to **increase our actual service for God**. Let us do what we have been doing of Christian teaching, visiting, and so on. However, in all let us do more, give more, and labor more. Who among us is working at his utmost or giving at his utmost? Let us quicken our speed. Suppose we are already doing so much that all the time we can possibly spare is fully occupied. Let us do what we do better. In some Christian churches, they do not want more ministries, but need more force put into them. You may skip over the seashore sand and scarcely leave an impression, but if you take heavy steps there is a deep footprint each time. May we in our service for God tread heavily and leave deep footprints on the sands of time.

"Whatsoever ye do, do it heartily, as to the Lord" (Colossians 3:23). Throw yourselves into it; do it with all your might. *"Thou shalt love the Lord thy God with all thine heart, and with all thy soul, and with all thy might"*

(Deuteronomy 6:5). Oh, to be enabled to serve God after this fashion—this would be to praise Him more and more!

Though I do not say that you can always tell how far a man praises God by the quantity of work that he does for God, yet it is not a bad gauge. It was an old aphorism of Hippocrates, the ancient physician, that you could judge a man's heart by his arm, by which he meant that by his pulse he judged of his heart. As a rule, though there may be exceptions, you can tell whether a man's heart beats truly for God by the work that he does for God. You who are doing much, do more; and you who are doing little, multiply that little, I pray you, in God's strength, and so praise Him more and more.

We could praise God much more if we threw more of His praise into **our common conversation**—if we spoke more of Him when we are out and about or when we sit at home. We could praise him more and more if we fulfilled our consecration and obeyed the precept, *"Whether therefore ye eat, or drink, or whatsoever ye do, do all to the glory of God."* (1 Corinthians 10:31).

We would do well if we added to our godly service **more singing**. The world sings. The millions have their songs. I must say the taste of the populace is a very remarkable taste just now as to its favorite songs. Many of them are so absurd and meaningless as to be unworthy of an idiot. Yet these things will be heard from men, and places will be thronged to listen to the stuff. Now, why should we—with the grand psalms we have of David, with the noble hymns of Cowper, Milton, and Watts—why should not we sing as well as they? Let us sing the songs of Zion. They are as cheerful as Sodom's songs. Let us drown out the howling nonsense of Gomorrha with the melodies of the New Jerusalem.

Finally, I desire that every Christian here would labor to be impressed with the importance of the subject which I have tried to bring before you. *"I will yet praise thee more and more."* Why, some of you have never praised God at all! Suppose you were to die today—and soon you must—where would you go? To heaven? What would heaven be to you? There can be no heaven for you. They praise God in the only heaven I have ever heard of. The environment of heaven is gratitude, praise, and adoration. You do not know anything of this, and therefore it would not be possible for God to make a heaven for you. God can do all things except make a sinful spirit happy, or violate truth and justice.

You **must either praise God or be miserable**. You do have a choice: you must either worship the God that made you, or else you must be wretched. It is not that He kindles a fire for you or casts on it the brimstone of His wrath, but your wretchedness begins within yourself, for to be unable to praise is to be full of hell. To praise God is heaven. When immersed in adoration, we are completely filled with felicity, but to be totally devoid of gratitude is to be totally devoid of happiness.

O that a change might come over you who have never blessed the Lord, and may it happen today! May the work of regeneration take place now! There is power in the Holy Spirit to change your heart of stone in a moment into a heart of flesh, so that instead of being cold and lifeless, it will palpitate with gratitude. Do you not see Christ on the cross dying for sinners? Can you look on that disinterested love and not feel some gratitude for such love as is there exhibited? Oh, if you but look to Jesus and trust Him, you will feel a flash of life come into your soul. With it will come praise, and then you will find it possible to begin the happy life. As you praise God more and more, so will that happy life be expanded and perfected in bliss.

But Christians, the last word is for you. Are you praising God more and more? If you are not, I am afraid of one thing: that you are probably praising Him less and less. It is a certain truth that **if we do not go forward in the Christian life, we go backward**. You cannot stand still. There is a drift one way or the other. Now, he that praises God less than he did, and goes on to praise Him less tomorrow, and less the next day, and so on—where will he go, and what is he? Evidently he is one of those that draw back unto perdition, and there are no persons on whom a more dreadful sentence is pronounced, often spoken of by Paul, and most terribly by Peter and Jude: *"Trees whose fruit withereth, without fruit, twice dead, plucked up by the roots...wandering stars for whom is reserved the blackness of darkness forever"* (Jude 1:12-13). It would have been infinitely better for them not to have known the way of righteousness, than having known it, after a fashion, to have turned aside! Better never to have put their hands to the plow, than having done so, to turn back from it.

But, beloved, I am persuaded of better things for you, things that accompany salvation, though I write so. I pray that God will lead you on from strength to strength, for that is the path of the just. May you grow in grace, for life is proven by growth. May you march like pilgrims towards heaven, singing all the way. The lark may serve us as a final picture, and an example of what we all should be. We should be mounting. Our prayer should be, "Nearer, my God, to Thee." Our motto might well be, "Higher! Higher! Higher!" As we mount, we should sing, and our song should grow louder, clearer, more full of heaven. Upward, sing as you soar. Upward, sing until you are dissolved in glory. Amen.

Chapter 3

Morning and Evening Songs

"To shew forth thy lovingkindness in the morning, and thy faithfulness every night."
—*Psalm 92:2*

The rabbis have a notion that this psalm was sung by Adam in paradise. There are no reasons why we should believe it was so, and there are a great many why we should be sure it was not. It is not possible that Adam could have sung concerning brutish men and fools, and the wicked springing up as grass, while as yet he was the only man and himself unfallen. Still, at least the first part of the psalm might have come as suitably from the lips of Adam as from our tongues. If Milton could put into Adam's mouth this language:

"These are thy glorious works, Parent of good,
    Almighty; thine this universal frame.
Thus wondrous fair, thyself how wondrous then!"

Milton might with equal fitness have made Adam say, *"It is a good thing to give thanks unto the Lord, and to sing praises unto thy name, O Most High: to shew forth thy lovingkindness in the morning, and thy faithfulness every night; for thou, Lord, hast made me glad through thy work: I will triumph in the works of thy hands"* (Psalm 92:1-4).

The Jews have for a long while used this psalm in the synagogue worship on their Sabbath. Very suitable it is for Sabbath, not so much in appearance, for there is little or no allusion to any sabbath rest in it, but because on that day above all others, our thoughts should be lifted up from all earthly things to God Himself. The psalm tunes the mind to adoration and so prepares it for Sunday worship. It supplies us with a noble subject for meditation—the Lord, the Lord alone—lifting us up even above His works into a contemplation of Himself and His mercies toward us. Oh, that always on the Sunday when we come together, we might assemble in the spirit of praise, feeling that it is good to give thanks unto the name of the Most High! I pray that always whenever we assemble together with other believers, we could say, *"Thou, Lord, hast made me glad through thy work: I will triumph in the works of thy hands."*

There is no doubt that in this second verse there is an allusion to the offering of the morning and the evening lambs. In addition to the great Paschal celebration once a year, and the other feasts and fasts, each of which brought Christ prominently before the mind of those Jews who were instructed by the Spirit of God, a lamb was offered every morning and every evening, as if to remind them that they needed daily cleansing for daily sin. At that time there was always a remembrance of sin, seeing that the one great sacrifice which puts away sin forever had not yet been offered. (See Hebrews 10:3-12.) Though now we need no morning or evening lamb and the very idea of a repetition or a rehearsal of the sacrifice of Christ is to us most horribly profane and blasphemous, yet we should remember continually the one perfect sacrifice and never wake in the morning without beholding *"the Lamb of God which taketh away the sin of the world"* (John 1:29), nor fall asleep at night without turning our eyes anew to Him who on the bloody tree was made sin for us.

Our text, however, is meant to speak to us concerning praise. Praise should be the continual exercise of believers. It is the joyful work of heaven. It should be the continual joy of earth. We are taught by the text, I think, that while praise should be given only to the One who is in heaven, and we should adore perpetually our triune God, yet there should be variety in our unity. We bless the Lord only. We have no music but for Him, but we do not always praise Him in the same fashion. As there were different instruments of music—the tambourine, the psaltery, the harp—so, too, there are different subjects, a subject for the morning and a subject for the evening; loving-kindness to be shown forth at one time, and faithfulness to be sung about at another. I wish that men studied more the praise they profess to present unto God.

I sometimes find, even in our public worship, simple as it is, that there is a lack of thought evidently among us. Time is not maintained with the precision which would grow out of thoughtfulness. There is a tendency to sing more slowly, as if devotion were wearying, if not wearisome. Too frequently I fear the singing gets to be mechanical, as if the tune had mastered the singer, and the praiser did not govern the tune by making those inflections and modulations of voice which the sense would suggest, if sung with all the heart and with the understanding also.

The very posture of some people indicates that they are going through the hymn, but the hymn is not going through their hearts, nor ascending to God on the wings of soaring gratitude. I have also noticed with sadness the way in which, if there happens to be a chorus at the close—a "Hallelujah" or "Praise God"—some will drop into their seats as if they had not thought enough to recollect that it was coming, and then, with a jerk and all confused, they stand up again, being so asleep in heart that anything out of the ordinary routine is too much for them. Far am I from caring for postures or tones, but when they indicate lack of heart, I do care, and so should you. Remember well that there is no more music to God's ear in any service than there is of heart-love and holy devotion. You may make floods of music with your organ if you like, or you may make equally good music—and some of us think even better—with human voices, but it is not music to God, either of instrument or voice, unless the heart is there. Further, the heart is not fully there nor the whole man unless the soul glows with praise.

In our private praise, also, we ought to think more of what we are doing, and concentrate our entire energies on this sacred exercise. Ought we not to sit down before we pray and ask ourselves, "What am I going to pray for? I bow my knee at my bedside to pray: ought I not to pause and consider the things I ought to ask for? What do I want and what are the promises which I should plead and why is it that I may expect that God should grant me what I want?" Would we not pray better if we spent more time in consideration?

When we come to praise we ought not to rush into it helter-skelter, but engage in it with prepared hearts. I notice that when musicians are about to perform, they tune their instruments. There is also a preparation of themselves in rehearsals before they perform their music in public. So our souls ought to rehearse the subject for which they are about to bless God. We ought to come before the Lord, both in public and in private, with subjects of praise which our thoughts have considered—not offering unto the Lord that which has cost us nothing, but with a warm heart pouring out before His throne adoration based on subjects of thanksgiving appropriate to the occasion. So it seems the psalmist would have us do: *"To shew forth thy lovingkindness in the morning and thy faithfulness every night."* It is not mere praise, but varied praise, praise with distinct subjects at appointed seasons.

Let us first consider from the text the **subject of morning worship**. Secondly, we will focus **another for evening devotion**. Both we need to **practice**.

First, then, notice morning worship: *"To show forth thy lovingkindness in the morning."* There cannot be a more suitable time for praising God than in the morning. Everything around is **congenial** then. Even in this great wilderness of brick and wood in which we live, the gleams of sunlight in these summer mornings seem like songs, songs without words, or rather music without sounds. Out in the country, when every blade of grass twinkles with its own drop of dew, all the trees glisten as if they were lit up with sapphires by the rising dawn, and a thousand birds awake to praise their Maker in harmonious concerts, with all their hearts all casting their entire energies into the service of holy song, it seems most fit that the key of the morning should be in the hand of praise. When the daylight lifts its eyelid, it should look out upon grateful hearts. We ourselves have newly risen from our beds, and if we are in a right state of mind we are thankful for the night's sleep.

> "The evening rests our wearied head,
>   And angels guard the room:
> We wake, and we admire the bed
>   That was not made our tomb."

Every morning is a sort of **resurrection**. At night we lay down to sleep, stripped of our garments, as our souls will be of their bodily array when we come to die, but the morning wakes us. If it be a Sunday morning we do not put on our workday clothes, but find our Sunday dress ready at hand. Even so will we be satisfied when we wake up in our Master's likeness, no more to put on the soiled raiment of earth, but to find it transformed into a Sunday robe in which we will be beautiful and fair, even as Jesus our Lord Himself. Now, as every morning brings to us, in fact, a resurrection from what might have been our tomb and delivers us from the image of death which through the night we wore, it ought to be saluted with thanksgiving. As the great resurrection morning will be awakened with the sound of the trumpet's far-sounding music, so let every morning, as though it were a resurrection to us, awaken us with hymns of joy.

> "All praise to thee who safe hast kept
> And hast refreshed me while I slept.
> Grant, Lord, when I from death shall wake
> I may of endless life partake."

"To show forth thy lovingkindness in the morning." We are **full of vigor** then. We will be tired before night comes round. Perhaps in the heat of the day we will be exhausted. Let us take care, while we are fresh, to give the cream of the morning to God. Our poet says:

> "The flower, when offered in the bud,
> Is no mean sacrifice."

Let us give the Lord the bud of the day, its virgin beauty, its unsullied purity. Say what you will about the evening—and there are many points about it which make it an admirable season for devotion—yet the morning is the **choice time**. Is it not a queenly hour? See how it is adorned with diamonds more pure than those which flash in the crowns of eastern potentates. The old proverb declares that they who would be rich must rise early. Surely those who would be rich towards God must do so. No dews fall in the middle of the day, and it is hard to keep up the dew and freshness of one's spirit in the worry, care, and turmoil of midday. But in the morning the dew should fall upon our fleece until it is saturated. It is well to wring it out before the Lord and give Him our morning's vigor, our morning's freshness and zeal.

You will see, I think, without my enlarging, that there is a fitness in the morning for praising God. But I will not merely confine the text to the morning of each day, because the same fitness pertains to the **morning of our days in total**. Our youth, our first hours of the day of life, ought to be spent in showing forth the loving-kindness of God. Dear young friends, you may rest assured that nothing can happen to you so blessed as to be converted while you are young. I bless God for my having known Him when I was fifteen years of age. However, I have often felt like that Irishman who said that he was converted at twenty, and he wished it had been twenty-one years before. I have often felt the same desire. Oh, if it could have been that the very first breath one drew had been consecrated to God, that it had been possible for the first rational thought to be one of devotion, that the first act of judgment had been exercised upon divine truth, and the first pulsing of affection had been towards the Redeemer who loved us and gave Himself for us! What blessed reflections would fill the space now occupied with penitent regrets. The first part of a Christian life has charms peculiar to itself. In some respects:

"That age is best which is the first,
For then the blood is warmer."

I know the later part of life is riper and more mellow. There is a sweetness about autumn fruit, but the basket of early fruit—the first ripe fruit—this is what God desires. Blessed are they who *"shew forth the loving-kindness of God in the morning!"*

The words may also be explained mystically to signify those **periods of life which are bright like the morning** to us. We have our ups and downs, our ebbs and flows, our mornings and our nights. Now, it is our duty and the privilege during our bright days for us to show forth God's loving-kindness in them. It may be some of you have had so rough a life that you consider your nights to be more numerous than your days. Others of us could not, even in common honesty, subscribe to such a belief. No, blessed be God, our mornings have been very numerous. Our days of joy and rejoicing, after all, have been abundant—infinitely more abundant than we might have expected they could be, dwelling as we do in the land of sorrows. Oh, when the joyous days are here, let us always consecrate them by showing forth God's loving-kindness.

Do not do as some do, who, if they are prospering, make a point of not owning to it. If they make money, for instance—well, they are "doing pretty well." "Pretty well," do they call it? There was a time, when if they had been doing half as well, they would have been ready to jump for joy. How often the farmer, when his crop could not be any larger, and when the field is loaded with it, will say, "Well, it is a very fair crop." Is that all that can be said? What robbery of God! This talk is far too common on all sides and ought to be most solemnly rebuked. When we have been enjoying a long stretch of joy, peace, and prosperity, instead of saying that it is so, we speak as if God has dealt very well with us on the whole, but at the same time He has done for us nothing very remarkable.

I saw a tombstone the other day which pleased me. I do not know that I ever saw an epitaph of that kind before. I think it was for a woman who died at the age of eighty. The inscription said of her, "who after a happy and grateful enjoyment of life, died." Now, that is what we ought to say, but we talk as if we were to be pitied for living, as if we were little better off than toads under a plow or snails in a tub of salt. We whine as if our lives were martyrdoms and every breath a woe. But it is not so. Such conduct slanders the good Lord. Blessed be the Lord for creating us. Our life has mercies, yes, innumerable mercies. Notwithstanding the sorrows and the troubles of it, there are joys and benedictions beyond all counting. There are mornings in which it becomes us to show forth the loving-kindness of the Lord. See, then, the season, the morning of each day, the morning of our days, and the morning of our brightness and prosperity.

The psalmist suggests that **the best topic for praise on such occasions is lovingkindness**. Truly I confess that this is a theme which might suit nights as well as days, although no doubt he saw an appropriateness in allotting this topic to the morning. Truly it might suffice for all day long. Was there ever such a word in any language as that word *"lovingkindness"*? I have sometimes heard Frenchmen talking about their language, and I have no doubt it is a very beautiful tongue. Germans glorify the speech of the Fatherland. I have heard our Welsh friends extolling their unpronounceable language, declaring it as the very tongue that was spoken in paradise—very likely indeed. But I venture to say that no language beneath the sky has a word in it that is richer than this, *"lovingkindness."*

It is a **dual deliciousness**. Within it are long chains of sweetnesses linked together. *"Lovingkindness"* is the kind of word with which to cast spells that should charm away all fears. It was said of Mr. Whitefield that he could have moved an audience to tears by saying the word "Mesopotamia." I think he could have done it better with *"loving-kindness."* Put it under your tongue now. Let it lie there. *"Lovingkindness."* Kindness. Does that mean "kinned-ness"? Some say "kinned-ness" is the root sense of the word—such feeling as we have to our own kin, for blood is ever thicker than water, and we act towards those who are our kindred as we cannot readily do towards strangers. Now, God has made us His kin. In His own dear Son He has taken us into His family. We are children of God: *"heirs of God and joint-heirs with Christ Jesus."* There is a "kinned-ness" from God to us through our great kinsman Jesus Christ.

But then the word is only half understood when you get to that, for it is loving-kindness. For a surgeon to set a man's limb when it is out of joint or broken is kindness, although he may do it somewhat roughly and in an off-hand manner. But if he does it very tenderly, covering the lion's heart with the lady's hand, then he shows loving-kindness. A man is picked up on the battlefield, put into an ambulance, and carried to the hospital. That is kindness. But if that poor soldier's mother could come into the hospital and see her boy suffering, she would show him loving-kindness, which is something far more. A child run over in the street and taken to the hospital would be cared for, I have no doubt, with the greatest kindness. However, after all, send for the child's mother, for she will give it loving-kindness. Just so the Lord deals with us. He gives us what we want in a fatherly manner. He gives to us what we need in the tenderest fashion. It is kindness; it is "kinned-ness." But it is also the **combination**

of the two: it is loving-kindness. The very heart of God seems written out in this word. We could hardly apply it in full force to any but to our Father who is in heaven.

Now, here is a subject for us to sing about in the morning. Where should I begin, with the hope of covering this subject? It is an endless one. Loving-kindness begins—I must correct myself—it never did begin. It had no beginning. *"I have loved thee with an everlasting love; therefore with lovingkindness have I drawn thee"* (Jeremiah 31:3). **Everlasting love**, therefore, is what we must begin to sing of. That everlasting love was infinite in its preparations: before we had been created, the Lord had made a covenant on our account and resolved to give His only begotten Son, that we might be saved from wrath through Him. The loving-kindness of God our Father appeared in Jesus Christ. Oh, let us always be talking about this!

I wonder why it is, when we meet each other, that we do not begin at once to say, "Have you been thinking over the loving-kindness of the Lord in the gift of His dear Son?" Indeed, it is such a marvelous thing that it ought not to be a nine-days' wonder with us. It ought to fill us with astonishment every day of our lives. Now, if something wonderful happens, everybody's mouth is full of it. We speak to one another about it at once, while, like the Athenians, all our neighbors are anxious to hear. Let our mouths, then, be full of the marvelous loving-kindness of God. For fear that we might leave the tale half untold, let us begin early in the morning to rehearse the eternal love manifested in the great gift of Jesus Christ.

If we have already spoken about these things and wish for variety, let us speak concerning the loving-kindness of God to each one of us in bringing us to Jesus. What a history each man's own life is. I suppose that if any one of our lives should be fully recorded, it would be more wonderful than a romance. I have sometimes seen a sunset of which I have said. "Now, if any painter had depicted that, I would have declared that the sky never looked in that way, it is so strange and unique." In the same way, should some of our lives have been fully written out, many would say, "It could not have been so." How many have said of Huntingdon's "Bank of Faith," for instance, "Oh, it is a bank of nonsense." Yet I believe that it is correct and bears the marks of truth upon its very face. I believe that the man did experience all that he has written, though he may not always have told us everything in the best possible manner. Many other people's lives would be quite as wonderful as his if they could be written down. Tell, then, of God's loving-kindness to yourself specially. Rehearse, if to no other ear than your own, and to the ear of God, the wondrous story of how:

"Jesus sought you when a stranger
Wandering from the fold of God."

Tell how His grace brought you to Himself
and so into eternal life. Then, sing of the loving-kindness of God to yourself since your new
birth. Remember the mercies of God. Do not
bury them in the grave of ingratitude. Let
them glisten in the light of gratitude. I am sure
that you will find this a blessed morning portion that will sweeten the whole day. The
psalmist would have you begin the day with it,
because you will need the entire day to complete it. Indeed, you will need all the days of
life and all eternity. I am half of Addison's
mind—though the expression is somewhat
hyperbolic:

"But, oh, eternity's too short
To utter half thy praise."

What a blessed subject you have before
you—the loving-kindness of the Lord—not
yourself. That is a horrible subject to speak
about. When I hear believers get up and glory
in their own attainments and graces, I remember the words of the wise man, *Let another
praise thee, and not thine own mouth*"
(Proverbs 27:2). Above all things, when a man
says that he has made great advances in sanc-
tification, it is sickening and clearly proves
that he has not learned the meaning of the

word, "humility." I hope the eyes of some of our friends will be opened, and that they will come to loathe the devil's meat which now deceives them. **May spiritual self-conceit be shunned as a deadly evil**, and may we no longer see it held up among us as a virtue. No, let our mouths be filled with God's praise, but not with our own.

Let not our tongues be always occupied with our griefs, either. If you have a skeleton in your house, why should you always invite every friend who calls upon you to inspect the uncomely thing? No, instead tell what God has done for you and of His loving-kindness. I have heard—and I repeat the story because it ought to be repeated, simple as it is—of a pastor who frequently called on a poor, bedridden woman who very naturally always told him of her pains and her wants. He knew all about her rheumatics: he had heard of them fifty times. At last he said to her, "My dear sister, I sympathize with you deeply, and I am never at all tired of hearing your complaints, but could you not now and then tell me something about what the Lord does for you—something about your enjoyments, how He sustains you under your pain, and so on?" It was a rebuke well put and well taken. Ever afterwards there was **less said about the griefs and more heard about the blessings**. Let us resolve, great God, *"To shew forth thy lovingkindness in the morning."*

Thus we have considered the time, morning, and the topic, loving-kindness. Now we are bound to observe the **manner** in which we are to deal with the subject. The psalmist says we are to **show it forth**, by which I suppose he means that we are not to keep to ourselves what we know about God's loving-kindness.

Every Christian in the morning ought to show it forth first **in his own bedroom** before God. He should express his gratitude for the mercies of the night and the mercies of his whole life. Then let him if it be possible, show it forth **in his family**. Let him gather them together and worship the Lord, and bless Him for His loving-kindness. And then when the Christian goes **into the world**, let him show forth God's loving-kindness. I do not mean by talking of it to every one he meets, casting pearls before swine as it would be to some men, but by the very way in which he speaks, acts, and looks.

A Christian ought to be the most cheerful of men, so that others would say, "What makes him look so happy? He is not rich. He is not always in good health. He has his troubles, but he seems to bear all so well and to trip lightly along the pathway of life." By our cheerful conversation we ought to show forth in the morning God's loving-kindness. "Ah," says one, "but what about when you are depressed in spirit?" Do not show it if you can help it. Do as your Master said, *"Appear not unto men to fast"* (Matthew 6:18). Do not imagine that the appearance of sadness indicates sanctity—it often means hypocrisy. To conceal one's own griefs for the sake of cheering others implies a self-denying sympathy which is the highest kind of Christianity.

Let us present the sacrifice of praise in whatever company we may be. But when we get among God's own people, then is the time for a whole burnt offering. Among our own kin we may safely open our box of sweets. When we find a brother who can understand the loving-kindness of the Lord, let us tell it forth with sacred delight. We have choice treasures which we cannot show to ungodly eyes, for they would not appreciate them. But when we meet with eyes which God has opened, then let us open the treasure chest and say, "Brother, rejoice in what God has done for us. See His loving-kindness to me His servant, and His tender mercies which have been ever of old."

Thus, beloved friends, I have set before you a good morning's work. I think, if God's Spirit helps us to attend to it, we will come out of our rooms with our breath smelling sweet with the praises of God. We will go into the world without care, much more without anger. We will go calmly to our work and meet our cares quietly and happily. The joy of the Lord will be our strength. **A good rule is never to look into the face of man in the morning until you have looked into the face of**

God. An equally good rule is always to have business with heaven before you have any business with earth. Oh, it is a sweet thing to bathe in the morning in the love of God—to bathe in it, so that when you come forth out of the ivory chambers of communion where you have been made glad, your garments will smell of the myrrh and aloes and cassia of holiness.

Do we all attend to this? I am afraid we are in too much of a hurry, or we get up too late. Could not we rise a little earlier? If we could steal even a few minutes from our beds, those few minutes would scatter their influence over the entire day. It is always bad to start on a journey without having checked the harness and the horse's shoes. Just so, it often happens that the time saved by omitting examination turns out to be a dead loss when the traveler has advanced a little on his journey. Not one minute, but a hundred minutes may be lost by the lack of a little attention at first. **Set the morning watch with care**, if you would be safe through the day. Begin well if you would end well. Take care that the helm of the day is set right toward the point you want to sail to, then whether you make much progress or little, it will be that far in the right direction. The morning hour is generally the index of the day.

Now let us turn to the second part of our subject. The psalmist says, *"To show forth... thy faithfulness every night."*

The night, beloved, is a particularly **choice time for praising God's faithfulness**. "Oh," says one, "I am very tired." Well, that may be, but it is a pity that we should be reduced to such a condition that we are too tired to praise God. A holy man of God used always to say, when they said to him, "Can you pray?" "Thank God, I am never too tired to pray." If anything can arouse us, the service of Christ should do it. There should be within us an enthusiasm which kindles at the very thought of prayer. Have you never known an army on the march, weary and ready to drop, but the band played some enlivening tune which has stirred the men until they have gone over the last few miles as they could not have done if it had not been for the inspiration of the refrain? Let the thought of praising God wake up our wearied energies, and let not God be robbed of His glory at the close of the day.

The close of the day is calm, quiet, and fit for devotion. God walked in the garden in the cool of the day, before man fell, and Adam went forth to meet Him. Isaac walked in the fields in the evening, and there he received a blessing. The evening is the sabbath of the day and should be the Lord's.

Now, notice the topic which is set for the evening: it is faithfulness. Why? Because we have had a little more experience with our God. We have **a day's more experience** than we had in the morning. Therefore we have more power to sing of God's faithfulness. We can look back now upon the day and see promises fulfilled. May I ask you to look over today? Can you not notice some promises which God has kept towards you? Show forth His faithfulness, then. **Provision** has been given you. He promised to give it; He has given it. **Protection** has been afforded you, more than you know of, infinitely more. **Guidance** also has been given in points where you otherwise would have gone very much astray. **Illumination** has been granted to you, and **comfort** also in a season of depression, as well as upholding in a time of temptation. God has given you much today. If He has taken anything away from you, yet still bless His name. It was only what He had given, and He had a right to take it. Look through the day, and you will find that God has acted towards you as He promised that He would act. You have had trouble, you say. Did not He say, *"In the world ye shall have tribulation"* (John 16:33)? Has He not spoken concerning the rod of the covenant? Affliction only illustrates His faithfulness.

Carefully observe the fulfilled promises of each day. It is a good custom to **conclude the day by rehearsing its special mercies**. I do not believe in keeping a detailed diary of each day's exents, for one is apt, for lack of something to put down, to write what is not true, or at least not real. I believe there is nothing more stilted or untruthful, generally, than a religious diary. It easily degenerates into self-deceit. Still, most days, if not all our days, reveal singular instances of providence, if we will but recognize them. Master Flavel used to say, "He that notices providences shall never be without a providence to notice." I believe we let our days glide by us, unobservant of the wondrous things that are in them and so miss many enjoyments. The uneducated person sees but little beauty in the wild flowers:

> "The primrose by the river's brim,
>   A yellow primrose it is to him
> And it is nothing more."

We, for lack of thought, let great mercies go by us. They are trifles to us and nothing more. Oh, let us change our ways, and think more of what God has done. Then we will utter a song concerning His faithfulness every night.

Do you notice in the text that word *"every."* It does not say, *"to shew forth his lovingkindness* [every] *morning,"* although it means that. No, concerning the nights it is very distinct: *"And his faithfulness every night."* It is a cold night. Did He not promise winter? Now it has come. The cold only proves His faithfulness. It is a dark night, but then it is a part of His covenant that there should be nights as well as days. Supposing that there were no nights and no winters, where would the covenant which God made with the earth be? But every change of temperature in the beautiful vicissitudes of the year, and every variation of light and shade, only illustrate the faithfulness of God. If you happen now to be full of joy, you can tell of divine faithfulness in rendering love and mercy to you. But if, on the other hand, you are full of trouble, tell of God's faithfulness, for now you have an opportunity of proving it. He will not leave you. He will not forsake you. His word is, *"When thou passest through the waters I will be with thee: and through the rivers, they shall not overflow thee"* (Isaiah 43:2). Depend upon it that this promise will be faithfully fulfilled.

Beloved friends, you who are getting old are nearing the **night of life**, you are specially fitted to show forth the Lord's faithfulness. The young people may tell of His loving-kindness, but **older people must tell of His faithfulness**. You can speak of forty or fifty years of God's grace to you, and you can confidently affirm that He has not once failed you. He has been true to every word that He has spoken. Now, I charge you, do not withhold your testimony. If young people should be silent, they are guilty, but they might speak, perhaps, another day. But for you advanced Christians to be silent will be sinful indeed, for you will not have another opportunity in this world of showing forth the faithfulness of God. Bear witness now, before your eyes are closed in death! The faithfulness of God every night is a noble subject for His gray-haired servants.

It truly is our great business to show forth His faithfulness. O beloved, do let us publish abroad the faithfulness of God. I wonder sometimes that there should be any doubts in the world about the doctrine of the final perseverance of the saints. I think the reason why there are any doubts is this: those professors who fall are very conspicuous, and everybody knows about them. If a high-flying professor makes a foul end of his boastings, why, that is talked of everywhere. They speak of it in Gath and publish it in the streets of Askelon. (See 2 Samuel 1:20.)

On the other hand, those thousands of true believers that stay on their course cannot, of course, say much about themselves. It would not be right that they would, but I wish they could sometimes say more about the unfailing goodness and immutable truthfulness of God, to **be a check to the effect produced by backsliders**. Then the world could know that the Lord does not cast away His people whom He did foreknow, but that He gives strength to them even in their fainting and bears them through. If there is any one topic that Christians ought to speak about thankfully, bravely, positively, continuously, it is the faithfulness of God to them. It is that on which Satan takes a dead aim in the minds of many tempted ones. Therefore, you should center the strength of your testimony on God's faithfulness, so that tried saints may know He does not forsake His people.

As a part of our own local congregations, let us **unitedly declare how faithful God has been!** The history of Metropolitan Tabernacle as a church has been very wonderful. When we were few and feeble, cast off and brought low, God appeared for us. Then we began to prosper, and we began also to pray. And what prayers they were! Surely the more we prayed the more God blessed us. We have now had almost twenty years of uninterrupted blessing. We have had no fits and starts, revivals and retreats, but onward has been our course. In the name of God, it has been a steady, continued progress, like the growth of a cedar upon Lebanon. Up to this time God has always heard prayer in this place. The very building which houses us was an answer to prayer. There is scarcely an institution connected with it that could not write upon its banner, "We have been blessed by a prayer-hearing God." It has become our habit to pray, and it is God's habit to bless us.

Oh, let us not grow weary and abate in our prayers or our praises! If we do, we will be limited in ourselves, but not in God. God will not leave us while we prove Him in His own appointed way. If we will continue steadily in earnest intercession and thanksgiving, our local churches may enjoy many more years of equal or greater prosperity, if so it pleases God. We have used no carnal attractions to gather people together to worship. We have procured nothing to please their tastes by way of elaborate music, fine dress, painted windows, processions, and the like. We have used the Gospel of Jesus without any rhetorical embellishments, simply spoken as a man speaks to a friend. God has blessed it, and He will bless it still.

Now, dear friends, each one of you can say of yourselves, as well as of the church, that God has been faithful to you. Tell it to your children. Tell them God will save sinners when they come to Him, for He saved you. Tell it to your neighbors. Tell them He is faithful and just to forgive us our sins if we confess them to Him, and to save us from all unrighteousness, for He forgave you. (See 1 John 1:9.) Tell every trembler you meet with that Jesus will in nowise cast out any that come to Him. (See John 6:37.) Tell all seekers that if they seek, they will find, and that to every one that knocks, the door of mercy will be opened. (See Matthew 7:7-8.) Tell the most despondent and despairing that Jesus Christ came into the world to save sinners, even the very chief. (See 1 Timothy 1:15.) Make known His faithfulness every night.

At the end, when your last night comes and you gather up your feet in the bed, like Jacob, **let your last testimony be centered**

on the Lord's faithfulness. Like glorious old Joshua, end your life by saying, *"Not one thing hath failed of all the good things which the LORD your God spake concerning you; all are come to pass"* (Joshua 23:14). The Lord bless you, dear friends, and grant that you all may know His loving-kindness and His faithfulness. Amen and Amen.

Chapter 4

Acceptable Praises and Vows

*"Praise waiteth for thee, O God, in Zion: and
unto thee shall the vow be performed.
O thou that hearest prayer,
unto thee shall all flesh come."*
—*Psalm 65:1-2*

Upon Zion was erected an altar dedicated to God for the offering of sacrifices. Except when prophets were commanded by God to break through the rule, burnt offering was to be offered only there. The worship of God upon the high places was contrary to the divine command: *"Take heed to thyself that thou offer not thy burnt offerings in every place that thou seest: but in the place which the Lord shall choose in one of thy tribes, there thou shalt offer thy burnt offerings, and there thou shalt do all that I command thee"* (Deuteronomy 12:13-14). Hence the tribes on the other side of Jordan, when they erected a memorial altar, disclaimed all intention of using it for the purpose of sacrifice. They said plainly, *"God forbid that we should rebel against the Lord, and turn this day from following the Lord, to build an altar for burnt offerings, for meat offerings, or for sacrifices, beside the altar of the Lord our God that is before his tabernacle"* (Joshua 22:29).

In fulfillment of this ancient type, we also *"have an altar whereof they have no right to eat which serve the tabernacle"* (Hebrews 13:10). Into our spiritual worship no observers of materialistic ritualism may intrude. They have no right to eat at our spiritual altar, and there is no other at which they can eat and live forever. There is but one altar—Jesus Christ our Lord. All other altars are impostors and idolatrous inventions. Whether of stone, wood, or brass, they are the toys with which those who have returned to the beggarly elements of Judaism amuse themselves, or else the apparatus with which clerical jugglers dupe the sons and daughters of men.

Holy places made with hands are now abolished. They were once the figures of the true, but now that the substance has come, the type is done away with. The all-glorious person of the Redeemer, God and Man, is the great center of Zion's temple and the only real altar of sacrifice. He is the church's Head, the church's Heart, the church's Altar, Priest, and All in All. *"To him shall the gathering of the people be"* (Genesis 49:10). Around Him we all congregate, even as the tribes did around the tabernacle of the Lord in the wilderness.

When the church is gathered together, we may compare it to the assemblies on Mount Zion, where the tribes of the Lord go up unto the testimony of Israel. There the song was raised, not so much from each separate worshipper as from all combined there. The praise as it rose to heaven was not only the praise of each one, but the praise of all. So where Christ is the center, where His one sacrifice is the altar on which all offerings are laid, and where the church unites around that common center rejoicing in that one sacrifice, there we find the true Zion. If we, who gather in Christ's name around His one finished sacrifice, present our prayers and praises entirely to the Lord through Jesus Christ, we are *"come unto Mount Zion, and unto the city of the living God, the heavenly Jerusalem, and to an innumerable company of angels, to the general assembly and church of the firstborn, which are written in heaven"* (Hebrews 12:22-23). This is Zion, even this house in the far-off islands of the Gentiles. We can say indeed, *"Praise waiteth for thee, O God, in Zion; and unto thee shall the vow be performed."*

We will, with devout attention, notice two things: the first is our holy worship which we desires to render, and then the stimulative encouragement which God provides for us, *"O thou that hearest prayer, unto thee shall all flesh come."* First, let us consider **the holy offering of worship** which we desire to present to God. It is twofold: there is praise, and there is also a vow, a **praise that waits**, and a **vow of which performance is promised**.

Let us think, first of all, of the praise. This is **the chief ingredient of the adoration of heaven**. What is thought to be worthy of that world of glory ought to be the main portion of the worship of earth. Although we will never cease to pray as long as we live here below and are surrounded by so many needs, yet we should never pray in such a way as to forget to praise. *"Thy kingdom come. Thy will be done on earth, as it is heaven"* (Matthew 6:10) must never be left out just because we are pressed with needs and, therefore, hasten to cry, *"Give us this day our daily bread."* It will be a sad hour when the worship of the church becomes only a solemn wail. Notes of exultant thanksgiving should always ascend from her solemn gatherings. *"Praise the Lord, O Jerusalem; praise thy God, O Zion"* (Psalm 147:12). *"Praise ye the Lord. Sing unto the Lord a new song, and his praise in the congregation of saints. Let Israel rejoice in him that made him: let the children of Zion be joyful in their King"* (Psalm 149:1-2). Let it abide as a perpetual ordinance, while sun and moon endure, *"Praise waiteth for thee, O God, in Zion."* Never think little of praise, since holy angels and saints made perfect count it their lifelong joy. Even the Lord himself said, *"Whoso offereth praise, glorifieth me"* (Psalm 50:23).

The tendency among us has been to undervalue praise as a part of public worship, whereas it should be second to nothing. We frequently hear of prayer meetings and but seldom of praise meetings. We acknowledge the duty of prayer by setting apart certain times for it, but we do not always so acknowledge the duty of praise. I hear of "family prayer," but do I ever hear of "family praise"? I know you cultivate private prayer, but are you as diligent also in private thanksgiving and secret adoration of the Lord? In everything we are to give thanks. It is as much a biblical precept as this one: *"In everything, by prayer and supplication with thanksgiving let your requests be made known unto God"* (Philippians 4:6).

I have often said that prayer and praise are like the breathing in and out of air and make up that **spiritual respiration** by which the inner life is instrumentally supported. We take in an inspiration of heavenly air as we pray; we breathe it out again in praise unto God from whom it came. If, then, we would be healthy in spirit, let us be abundant in thanksgiving. Prayer, like the root of a tree, seeks for and finds nutriment; praise, like the fruit, renders a revenue to the owner of the vineyard. Prayer is for ourselves; praise is for God. Let us never be so selfish as to abound in the one and fail in the other. Praise is a slender return for the boundless favors we enjoy. Let us not be slack in rendering it in our best music, the music of a devout soul. *"Praise the Lord; for the Lord is good: sing praises unto his name; for it is pleasant"* (Psalm 135:3).

Let us notice the praise which is mentioned in our text, which is to be a large matter of concern to the Zion of God whenever the saints are gathered together. You will first observe that it is praise **exclusively rendered to God**. *"Praise waiteth for thee, O God, in Zion."* May all the praise be for Him, with no praise for man or for any other who may be thought to be, or may pretend to be, worthy of praise. I have sometimes gone into places called houses of God where the praise has waited for a woman (the virgin), where praise has waited for the saints, where incense has smoked to heaven, and songs and prayers have been sent up to deceased martyrs and confessors who are supposed to have power with God. In Rome it is so, but in Zion it is not so. Praise waits for Mary in Babylon, but *"praise waiteth for thee, O God, in Zion."* Unto God, and God alone, the praise of His true church must ascend.

If protestants are free from this deadly error, I fear they are guilty of another, for in our worship **we too often minister to our own selves**. We do so when we make the tune and manner of the song more important than the substance of it. I am afraid that where organs, choirs, and soloists are left to do the praising for the congregation, men's minds are more occupied with the performance of the music than with the Lord, who alone is to be praised. God's house is meant to be sacred unto Himself, but too often it is made an opera house, and Christians form an audience, not an adoring assembly. The same thing may, unless great care is taken, happen amid the simplest worship, even though everything which does not taste of gospel plainness is excluded, for in that case we may drowsily drawl out the words and notes with no heart whatever. To sing with the soul, this only is to offer acceptable praise. We do not come together to amuse ourselves, to display our powers of melody, or our aptness in creating harmony. We come to pay our adoration at the footstool of the Great King, to whom alone be glory forever and ever. **True praise is for God and for God alone**.

You must take heed that the minister, who, above all, would reject a share of praise, is not set up as a demi-god among you. Refute practically the old slander that the presbyter is your only priest. Look higher than the pulpit, or you will be disappointed. Look above an arm of flesh, or it will utterly fail you. We may say of the best preacher on the earth, "Give God the praise, for we know that this man is a sinner." If we thought that you paid superstitious reverence to us, we would, like Paul and Silas, rend our clothes and cry, *"Sirs, why do ye these things? We also are men of like passions with you, and preach unto you that ye should turn from these vanities unto the living God, which made heaven, and earth, and the sea, and all things that are therein"* (Acts 14:15).

It is not to any man, to any priest, to any order of men, to any being in heaven or earth beside God, that we should burn the incense of worship. We would just as soon worship cats with the Egyptians, as popes with the Romanists. We see no difference between the people whose gods grew in their gardens and the sect whose deity is made by their baker. Such vile idolatry is to be loathed. To God alone shall all the praise of Zion ascend.

It is to be feared that some of our praise ascends nowhere at all, but it is as though it were scattered to the winds. We do not always believe and experience God. *"He that cometh to God must believe that he is, and that he is the rewarder of them that diligently seek him"* (Hebrews 11:6). This is as true of praise as of prayer. *"God is a Spirit, and they that* [praise] *him must* [praise] *him in spirit and in truth"* (John 4:24), for *"the Father seeketh such"* to praise Him. If we do not lift our eyes and our hearts to Him, we are but misusing words and wasting time. Our praise is not as it should be if it is not reverently and earnestly directed to the Lord of Hosts. Vain is it to shoot arrows without a target: we **must aim exclusively for God's glory** in our holy songs.

Note, next, that it should be **continual**. *"Praise waiteth for thee, O God, in Zion."* Some translators conceive that the main idea is that of continuance. It remains and abides; Zion does not break up when the assembly is gone. We do not leave the holiness in the building, for it never was in the stone and the timber, but only in the living assembly of the faithful:

> "Jesus, where'er thy people meet
>   There they behold thy mercy seat;
> Where'er they seek thee, you art found,
>   And every place is hallow'd ground.

> "For you within no walls confined
>   Inhabitest the humble mind;
> Such ever bring thee where they come
>   And going take thee to their home."

The people of God, as they **never cease** to be a church, should maintain the Lord's praise perpetually as a community. Their assemblies should begin with praise and end with praise, and ever be conducted in a spirit of praise. There should be in all our assemblies a spiritual incense altar, always smoking with *"the pure incense of sweet spices, according to the work of the apothecary"* (Exodus 37:29), the thanksgiving which is made up of humility, gratitude, love, consecration, and holy joy in the Lord. It should be for the Lord alone, and it should never go out day nor night.

"His mercy endureth forever" (Psalm 136:1). and so should our praises endure forever. He makes the dawning of the morning to rejoice. Let us celebrate the rising of the sun with holy psalm and hymn. He makes the closing in of the evening to be glad. Let Him have our vesper praise. *"One generation shall praise thy works to another, and shall declare thy mighty acts"* (Psalm 145:4). Could His mercy cease, there might be some excuse for holding back our praises. But, even should it seem to be so, men who love the Lord would say with Job, *"Shall we receive good at the hand of the Lord and shall we not also receive evil?...The Lord gave, and the Lord hath taken away; and blessed be the name of the Lord"* (Job 2:10; 1:21).

Let our praise abide, continue, remain and be perpetual. It was a good idea of Bishop Farrar, that, in his own house, he would keep up continual praise to God. As he had a large household which numbered twenty-four, he set apart each one for an hour in the day to be engaged especially in prayer and praise, that he might girdle the day with a circle of worship. We could not do that. To attempt it might on our part be superstition. However, to fall asleep blessing God, to rise in the night to meditate on Him, and when we wake in the morning to feel our hearts leap in the prospect of His presence during the day, this is attainable for us. We ought to strive to reach it.

It is much to be desired that all day long, in every avocation, and every recreation, the soul should **spontaneously pour forth** praise, even as birds sing, flowers perfume the air, and sunbeams cheer the earth. We would be incarnate praise enshrined in flesh and blood. From this delightful duty we would desire no cessation and ask no pause. *"Praise waiteth for thee, O God, in Zion."* Your praise may come and go from the outside world, where all things ebb and flow, for it lies beneath the moon, and there is no stability in it. But amid God's people, who dwell in Him and possess eternal life, in them His praise should perpetually abide.

A third point, however, is clear on the surface of the words. *"Praise waiteth for thee"* intimates that praise **must be humble**. The servants "wait" in the king's palace. There the messengers stand, equipped for any mission; the attendants tarry, prepared to obey; and the courtiers surround the throne, all eager to receive the royal smile and to fulfill the high command. Our praises ought to stand, like ranks of messengers, waiting to hear what God's will is, for this is to praise Him.

Furthermore, true praise lies in **the actual doing of the divine will**, even to the extent of pausing in sacred reverence until God the Lord speaks, whatever that will may be. It is true praise to wait subserviently on Him. Praises may be looked upon as servants who delight to obey their master's bidding. There is such a thing as an unholy familiarity with God. This age is not so likely to fall into it as some ages have been, for there is little familiarity with God of any sort now. Public worship has become more formal, stately, and distant. How seldom do we meet with the intense nearness to God which Luther enjoyed! But, however near we come to God, still He is God, and we are His creatures. Truly, He is *"our Father,"* but be it ever remembered that He is *"our Father which art in heaven."* *"Our Father"*—therefore He is near and intimate. *"Our Father in heaven"*—therefore we humbly, solemnly bow in His presence. There is a familiarity that runs into presumption. There is another familiarity which is so sweetly tempered with humility that it does not intrude. *"Praise waiteth for thee"* with a servant's uniform donned, a servant's ear to hear, and a servant's heart to obey. Praise bows at His footstool, feeling that it is still an unprofitable servant.

But, perhaps, you are aware, dear friends, that there are other translations of this verse. *"Praise waiteth for thee,"* may be read, "Praise is silent unto thee" or "is silent before thee." One of the oldest Latin commentators translates it, "Praise and silence belong unto thee." I am told that, in the King of Spain's Bible, it reads, "The praise of angels is only silence before thee, O Jehovah." When we do our best, **our highest praise is but silence before God**, and we must praise Him with confession of shortcomings. Oh, that we too, our poet puts it, might:

> "Loud as his thunders speak his praise,
>   And sound it lofty as his throne!"

But we cannot do that. When our notes are most uplifted and our hearts most joyous, we have not spoken all His praise. Compared to what His nature and glory deserve, our most earnest praise has been little more than silence. Oh, have you not often felt it to be so? Those who are satisfied with formal worship think that they have done well when the music has been correctly sung. However, those who worship God in spirit feel that they cannot magnify Him enough. They blush over the hymns they sing and retire from the assembly of the saints mourning that they have fallen far short of His glory.

O for an enlarged mind, rightly to conceive His divine majesty. Next, for the gift of utterance to clothe the thought in fitting language. Then, for a voice like many waters, to sound forth the noble strain. Alas! As yet, we are humbled at our failures to praise the Lord as we would like:

> "Words are but air, and tongues but clay,
>   And his compassions are divine."

How, then, shall we proclaim to men God's glory? When we have done our best, our praise is but silence before the merit of His goodness and the grandeur of His greatness. Yet it may be well to observe here that acceptable praise to God presents itself under a variety of forms. There is praise for God in Zion, and it is often spoken; but there is often praise for God in Zion, and it is silence. There are some who cannot sing vocally, but perhaps, before God, they sing best. There are some, I know, who sing very harshly and inharmoniously—that is to say, to our ears. Yet God may accept them rather than the noise of stringed instruments carefully touched.

There is a story told of Rowland Hill's being much troubled by a good old lady who would sit near him and sing with a most horrible voice very loudly—as those people generally do who sing badly. He at last begged her not to sing so loudly. But when she said, "It comes from my heart," the honest man of God retracted his rebuke and said, "Sing away. I should be sorry to stop you."

When praise comes **from the heart**, who would wish to restrain it? Even the shouts of the old Methodists, their "hallelujahs" and "glorys," when uttered in fervor, were not to be forbidden. for *"If these should hold their peace, the stones would immediately cry out"* (Luke 19:40). But there are times when those who sing, and sing well, have too much praise in their soul for it to enclose itself in words. Like some strong liquors which foam and swell until they burst each hoop that binds the barrel because they are narrowly vented, so it is that sometimes we want a larger channel for our souls than that of mouth and tongue. We long to have all our nerves and sinews made into harp strings and all the pores of our bodies made mouths of thankfulness. Oh, that we could praise with our whole nature, not one single hair of our heads or drop of blood in our veins keeping back from adoring the Most High! When this desire for praise is most vehement, we fall back upon silence and quiver with the adoration which we cannot speak. Silence becomes our praise.

"A sacred reverence checks our songs,
    And praise sits silent on our tongues."

It would be well, perhaps, in our public service, if we had more often the sweet relief of silence. I am persuaded that frequent silence is most beneficial. The occasional unanimous silence of all the saints when they bow before God would, perhaps, better express and more fully promote devout feeling than any hymns which have been composed or songs that could be sung. To make silence a part of worship habitually might be affection and formalism, but to include it occasionally, even frequently, into the service would be advantageous and profitable. Let us, then, by our silence, praise God, and let us always confess that our praise, compared with God's deserving, is but silence.

I would add that there is in the text the idea that **praise waits for God expectantly**. When we praise God, we expect to see more of Him soon and, therefore, wait for Him. We bless the King, but we desire to draw nearer to Him. We magnify Him for what we have seen, and we expect to see more. We praise Him in His outer courts for we will soon be with Him in the heavenly mansions. We glorify Him for the revelation of Himself in Jesus, for we expect to be like Christ and to be with Him where He is. When I cannot praise God for what I am, I will praise Him for what I shall be. When I feel dull and dead about the present, I will take the words of our delightful hymn and say:

> "And a new song is in my mouth,
>   To long-loved music set;
> Glory to thee for all the grace
>   I have not tasted yet."

My praise should not only be thanksgiving for the past, which is but discharging a debt of gratitude, but my faith needs to anticipate the future and wait upon God to fulfill His purposes. Then I will begin to pay my praise even before the mercy comes.

Let us for a moment present our praise to God, each one of us on his own account. We have our common mercies. We call them common, but, oh, how priceless they are. Health to be able to assemble together and not to be stretched on a bed of sickness, I count better than bags of gold. To have our reason and not to be confined in an asylum. To have our children still about us and dear relatives spared still to us. To have bread to eat and clothes to put on. To have been kept from defiling our character. To have been preserved today from the snares of the enemy! These are godlike mercies, and for all these our praises shall wait upon God.

Here I take up the thoughts suggested by the psalm itself in the next verse, and you will doubly praise God. *"Iniquities prevail against me. As for our transgressions, thou shalt purge them away"* (Psalm 65:3). Infinite love has made us completely clean, though we were black and filthy. We are washed—**washed in priceless blood**. Praise Him for this! Go on with the passage, *"Blessed is the man whom thou choosest and causest to approach unto thee"* (Psalm 65:4). Is not the blessing of access to God an exceeding choice one? Is it a light thing to feel that we, *"who sometimes were far off, are made nigh by the blood of Christ"* (Ephesians 2:13), because of **electing love**?

"Blessed is the man whom thou choosest." You who have been eternally chosen, can you

be silent? Has God favored you above others, and can your lips refuse to sing? No, you will magnify the Lord exceedingly, because He has chosen Jacob unto Himself and Israel for His peculiar treasure.

Let us read on and praise God that we have an abiding place among His people: *"That he may dwell in thy courts"* (Psalm 65:4). Blessed be God we are not to be cast forth and driven out after a while, but we have **a guaranteed inheritance** among the sons of God. We praise Him that we have the satisfaction of dwelling in His house as children. *"We shall be satisfied with the goodness of thy house, even of thy holy temple"* (Psalm 65:4). But I simply say to you, there are ten thousand reasons for taking down the harp from the willows. I know no reason for permitting it to hang there idle. There are ten thousand times ten thousand reasons for speaking well of *"Christ* [who] *hath loved us, and hath given himself for us"* (Ephesians 5:2).

"The Lord hath done great things for us whereof we are glad" (Psalm 126:3). I remember hearing in a prayer meeting this delightful verse mutilated in prayer, *"The Lord hath done great things for us whereof we* [desire to be] *glad."* Oh, how I dislike mauling, mangling, and adding to a text of Scripture. If we are to have the Scriptures revised, let it be by scholars and not by every ignoramus. "Desire to be glad" indeed? This is fine gratitude to

God when He *"hath done great things for us."*
If these great things have been done, our souls
must be glad and cannot help it. They must
overflow with gratitude to God for all His
goodness.

That covers the first part of our holy sacrifice. Attentively let us consider the second,
namely, the vow. *"Unto thee shall the vow be
performed."*

We are not given to **vow-making** in these
days. There was a time when it was done far
more often. It may be that had we been better
men we would have made more vows. It may
possibly be that had we been more foolish men
we would have done the same. The practice
was so abused by superstition that devotion
has grown half-ashamed of it. But most of us
have, at any rate, bound ourselves with occasional vows. I do confess a vow I have not kept
as I desire: the **vow made on my conversion**. I surrendered myself, body, soul, and
spirit to Him that bought me with a price, and
the vow was not made by way of excess of devotion or superfluously—it was but my reason-
able service. You have done that. Do you
remember the love of your betrothed, the time
when Jesus was very precious and you had just
entered into the marriage bond with Him? You
gave yourselves up to Him to be His forever
and forever. It is a part of worship to perform
that vow. Renew it now; make another surren-
der of yourselves to Him whose you are and

whom you serve. Say, *"Bind the sacrifice with cords, even with cords unto the horns of the altar"* (Psalm 118:27). Oh, for another thong to strap the victim to the altar horn! Does the flesh struggle? Then let it be more fastly bound, never to escape from the altar of God.

Beloved, many of us did, in effect, make a most solemn vow at the time of our baptism. We **were buried with Christ in baptism unto death**, and, unless we were greatly pretending, we vowed that we were dead in Christ and buried with Him. We also professed that we were risen with Him. Now, shall the world live in those who are dead to it, but shall Christ's life be absent from those who are risen with Him? We gave ourselves up there and then, in that solemn act of mystic burial. Recall that scene, I pray you. As you do so, blush and ask God that your vow may yet be performed. As Doddridge well expresses it:

> "Baptized into your Savior's death,
>   Your souls to sin must die;
> With Christ your Lord ye live anew,
>   With Christ ascend on high."

Some such vow we made, too, when we united ourselves to the church of God. There was an **understood compact between us and the church**, that we would serve it, that we would seek to honor Christ by holy living, increase the church by propagating the faith, seek its unity and comfort by our own love and sympathy with the members. We had no right to join with the church if we did not mean to give ourselves up to it, under Christ, to aid in its prosperity and increase. There was a stipulation made and a covenant understood, when we entered into communion and league with our family in Christ. How about that? Can we say that, as unto God and in His sight, the vow has been performed? Yes, we have been true to our covenant in a measure. Oh, that it were more fully so!

Some of us made another vow, when we gave ourselves, under divine call, wholly to the work of the **Christian ministry**. Though we have taken no orders and received no earthly ordination—for we are no believers in manmade priests—yet tacitly it is understood that the man who becomes a minister of the church of God is to give his whole time to his work and that his body, soul, and spirit should be thrown into the cause of Christ. Oh, that this vow were more fully performed by pastors of the church! Elders and deacons, when you accepted office, you knew what the church meant. She expected holiness and zeal of you. The Holy Ghost made you overseers so that you might feed the flock of God. Your office proves your obligation. You are practically under a vow. Has that vow been performed? Have you performed it in Zion unto the Lord?

Besides that, making vows has been the habit of godly men occasionally, in times of pain and losses. Does not this hymn put it so?

"Among the saints that fill thine house,
　　My offerings shall be paid;
There shall my zeal perform the vows,
　　My soul in anguish made.

"Now I am thine, forever thine,
　　Nor shall my purpose move!
Thy hand hath loosed my bands of pain
　　And bound me with thy love.

"Here in thy courts I leave my vow,
　　And thy rich grace record.
Witness, ye saints, who hear me now
　　If I forsake the Lord."

In times of affliction, you said, "If I am ever raised up, and my life is prolonged, it will be better spent." You said, also, "If I am delivered out of this great trouble, I hope to consecrate my substance more to God." Another time you said, "If the Lord will return to me the light of His countenance and bring me out of this depressed state of mind, I will praise Him more than ever before." Have you remembered all this? Recently having recovered from a sick bed, I admonish myself as well as you. I only wish I were a better hearer. Then I would exhort myself in this respect, saying, "I charge thee, my heart, to perform your vow."

Some of us, dear friends, have **made vows in time of joy**, the season of the birth of the firstborn child, the recovery of the wife from sickness, the merciful restoration that we have ourselves received, times of increasing goods, or seasons when the splendor of God's face has been unveiled before our wondering eye. Have we not made vows like Jacob did when he woke up from his wondrous dream, took the stone which had been his pillow, poured oil on its top, and made a vow unto the Most High? We have all had our Bethels. Let us remember that God has heard us, and let us perform unto Him the vows which our souls made in their time of joy.

However, I will not try to open the secret pages of your private notebooks. You have had tender passages, which you would not desire me to read aloud. If your life were written, you would say, "Let these not be told; they were only between God and my soul." They are some chaste and blessed love passages between you and Christ, which must not be revealed to men. Have you forgotten how then you said, *"I am my beloved's, and my beloved is mine"* (Song of Solomon 6:3)? What you promised when you saw all His goodness made to pass before you. I have now to stir up your pure minds by way of remembrance and bid you to present unto the Lord the **double offering of your heart's praise and of your per-formed vow**. *"O magnify the Lord with me,* *and let us exalt his name together"* (Psalm 34:3).

Now, I must include a few words about the blessed encouragement afforded us in the text for the presentation of these offerings unto God. Here it is: *"O you that hearest prayer. unto you shall all flesh come."* Observe, here, that God hears prayer. In some aspects, prayer is the lowest form of worship, and yet He accepts it. It is not the worship of heaven, and, in a measure, it is selfish. Praise is superior worship for it is elevating. It is the utterance of a soul that has received good from God and is returning its love to Him in acknowledgment. Praise has a sublime aspect.

Now, observe, if prayer is heard, then praise will be heard, too. If the lower form, on weaker wing as it were, reaches the throne of the Majesty on high, how much more shall the angelic wing of praise bear itself into the divine presence. Prayer is heard of God. Therefore, **our praises and vows will be heard**, also. This is a very great encouragement, because it seems terrible to pray when you are not heard and discouraging to praise God if He will not accept it. What would be the use of it? But if prayer and, even more so, praise are most surely heard, then let us continue and abide in thanksgiving. *"Whoso offereth praise glorifieth me, saith the Lord"* (Psalm 50:23).

Observe also according to the text, that all prayer, if it is true prayer, is heard of God, for so it is put: *"Unto thee shall all flesh come."* Oh, how glad I am at that word. My poor prayer—will God reject it? Yes, I might have feared so if He had said, "Unto Me shall all spirits come." Behold, beloved, He takes the grosser part as it were, and looks at prayer in His infinite compassion, perceiving it to be what it is—a feeble thing—a cry coming from poor, fallen flesh. Yet He puts it, *"Unto* [me] *shall all flesh come."* My broken prayer, my groaning prayer shall get to Him. Though it seems to me a thing of flesh, it is nevertheless inspired in me by His Spirit. My song, though my voice is hoarse and oftentimes my notes are most feeble, will reach Him. Though I groan because it is so imperfect, yet even that will come to Him. Prayer, if it is sincere, will be received by God, notwithstanding all its faultiness, through Jesus Christ. Then so it will be with our praises and our vows.

Again, prayer is always and habitually received of God. *"O thou that hearest prayer."* Not did hear it or on a certain occasion may have heard it, but He that **ever** hears prayer. If He always hears prayer, then He always hears praise. Is not this delightful to think that God does hear my praise—though it is but that of a child or a poor unworthy sinner—does accept it in spite of its imperfections, and does accept it always? Oh, I will have another hymn today. I will sing a new song tomorrow. I will forget my pain. I will forget for a moment all my care. If I cannot sing aloud because of those with me, yet will I set the bells of my heart ringing. I will make my soul full of praise. If I cannot let it out of my mouth, I will praise Him in my soul, because He always hears me.

You know it is hard to do things for one who never accepts what you do. Many a wife has said, "Oh! It is hard. My husband never seems pleased. I have done all I can, but he takes no notice of little deeds of kindness." But how easy it is to serve a person who, when you have done any little thing, says, "How kind it was of you," and thinks much of it. Ah, poor child of God, **the Lord thinks much of your praises, your vows, your prayers**. Therefore, do not be slack to praise and magnify Him unceasingly.

Further, we have not quite finished with that word, *"Unto thee shall all flesh come."* All flesh will come because the Lord hears prayer. Then all my praises will be heard, and all the praises of all sorts of men, if sincere, will come unto God. The great ones of the earth will present praise, and the poorest of the poor also, for He will not reject them.

Lord, would You put it so, *"Unto [Me] shall all flesh come,"* and yet would You say, "But not such a one as you?" Would You exclude me? Beloved, fear not that God will reject you. I am reminded of a good earnest believing woman, who in prayer said, "Lord, I am content to be the second You would forsake, but I

114

cannot be the first." The Lord says all flesh shall come to Him, and it is implied that He will receive them when they come—all sorts of men, all classes and conditions of men. Then **He will not reject** me if I come, nor my prayers if I pray, nor my praise if I praise Him, nor my vows if I perform them. Come then, let us praise the Lord. Let us worship and bow down. Let us kneel before the Lord our maker, for *"we are the people of his pasture and the sheep of his hand"* (Psalm 95:7).

Finally, beloved, there may be **difficulties in your way**. Iniquities may hinder you, or infirmities; but there is the promise, *"thou shalt purge them away"* (Psalm 65:3). Infirmities may check you, but note the word of divine help, *"Blessed is the man whom thou...causest to approach unto thee"* (Psalm 65:4). He will come to your aid and lead you to Himself. Infirmities, therefore, are overcome by divine grace.

Perhaps your **emptiness hinders** you. *"We shall be satisfied with the goodness of thy house"* (Psalm 65:4). It is not your goodness that is to satisfy either God or you, but God's goodness is to satisfy. Come, then, with your iniquity, come with your infirmity, come with your emptiness. Come if you have never come to God before. Come and confess your sin to God, and ask for mercy. You can do no less than ask. Come and trust His mercy which endures forever because it has no limit. Do not think hardly of Him, but come and lay down at His feet. If you perish, perish there. Come and tell your grief. Pour out your hearts before Him. Turn the vessel of your nature upside down, drain out the last dregs, and pray to be filled with the fullness of His grace. Come to Jesus. He invites you. He will enable you.

A cry from the back pew will reach the sacred ear. "But I have not prayed before," you say. Everything must have a beginning. Oh, that your beginning might come now. It is not because you pray well that you are to come, but because the Lord hears prayer graciously, therefore, all flesh shall come. You are welcome. None can block your way. Come! This is mercy's welcome hour.

May the Lord's bands of love be cast about you. May you be drawn now to Him. Come by way of the cross. Come resting in the precious atoning sacrifice, believing in Jesus. He has said, *"Him that cometh unto me, I will in no wise cast out"* (John 6:37). The grace of our Lord be with you. Amen.

Chapter 5

*The Power of Prayer &
the Pleasure of Praise*

*"Ye also helping together by prayer for us, that
for the gift bestowed upon us by the means of
many persons thanks may be given
by many on our behalf.
For our rejoicing in this, the testimony of our
conscience, that in simplicity and godly
sincerity, not with fleshly wisdom, but by the
grace of God, we have had our conversation in
the world, and more abundantly to you-ward."
—2 Corinthians 1:11-12*

The apostle Paul had, by unique providence, been delivered from imminent peril
in Asia. During the great riot at Ephesus,
Paul's life was greatly in jeopardy when De-
metrius and his fellow shrine-makers raised a
great tumult against him, because they saw
that their craft was in danger. Paul thus
wrote, *"We were pressed out of measure, above*

117

strength, insomuch that we despaired even of life" (2 Corinthians 1:8). The apostle attributes to God alone his preservation. If he referred also to the occasion when he was stoned and left for dead, there is much appropriateness in his blessing, *"God which raiseth the dead"* (v. 9).

Moreover, the apostle argued from the fact that God had thus delivered him in the past, was still his helper in the present, and that He would be with him also in the future. Paul is a master at all arithmetic. His faith was always a ready reckoner. We find him here computing by the **Believer's Rule of Three**: he argues from the past to the present, and from the present to things yet to come. The verse preceding our text is a brilliant example of this arriving at a comfortable conclusion by the Rule of Three: *"Who delivered us from so great a death, and does deliver: in whom we trust that he will yet deliver us"* (v. 10). Because God is *"the same yesterday, and today, and forever"* (Hebrews 13:8), His love in time past is an infallible assurance of His kindness today, and an equally certain pledge of His faithfulness tomorrow, whatever our circumstances may be, however perplexing may be our path, and however dark our horizon. If we argue by the rule of "He has, He does, He will," our comfort can never be destroyed. Take courage, afflicted one. If you had a changeable God to deal with, your soul might be full of bitterness. However, because He is *"the same yesterday, and today, and forever,"* every repeated manifestation of His grace should make it easier for you to rest in Him. Every renewed experience of His fidelity should confirm your confidence in His grace. May the blessed Spirit teach us to grow in holy confidence in our ever-faithful Lord.

Although Paul thus acknowledged God's hand, and God's hand alone, in his deliverance, yet he was not so foolish as to deny or undervalue the secondary causes. On the contrary, having first praised the God of all comfort, he then remembered with gratitude the earnest prayers of the many loving intercessors. Gratitude to God must never become an excuse for ingratitude to man. It is true that the Almighty shielded the apostle from the Gentiles, but He did it in answer to prayer. The chosen vessel was not broken by the rod of the wicked, for the out-stretched hand of the God of heaven was his defense.

However, that hand was outstretched because the people of Corinth and the saints of God everywhere had prevailed at the throne of grace by their united prayers. With gratitude those successful pleadings were mentioned in the text: *"Ye also helping together by prayer for us."* Paul desired the believers to unite their praises with his, *"that for the gift bestowed upon us by the means of many persons thanks may be given by many on our behalf."* He added that he had a claim on their love, since he was not as some who were unfaithful to their trust, but his conscience was clear that he had preached the Word simply and with sincerity.

We will, first, acknowledge **the power of unified prayer**; secondly, urge you to **praise in harmony with other believers**; and in the third place, **press our joyful claim upon you**—a claim which is not ours alone, but belongs to all ministers of God who in sincerity labor for souls.

First, then, dear friends, it is my duty and my privilege to acknowledge the power of united prayer. It has pleased God to make prayer the abounding and rejoicing river through which most of our choice mercies flow to us. It is the golden key which unlocks the well-stocked granaries of our heavenly Joseph. It is written upon each of the mercies of the covenant, *"I will yet for this be inquired of by the house of Israel to do it for them"* (Ezekiel 36:37). There are mercies which come unsought, for God is found by those that sought not for Him. But there are other favors which are only bestowed upon the men who ask, and therefore receive; who seek, and therefore find; who knock, and therefore gain an entrance.

Why God is pleased to command us to pray at all is not difficult to discover, for prayer glorifies God by putting man in **the humblest posture of worship**. In prayer the creature acknowledges his Creator with reverence, and confesses Him to be the Giver of every good and perfect gift. The eye is lifted up to behold the glory of the Lord, while the knee is bent to the earth in the lowly acknowledgment of weakness. Though prayer is not the highest mode of adoration (or otherwise it would be continued by the saints in heaven), yet it is the most humble, and so the most fitting, to set forth the glory of the perfect One as it is beheld by imperfect flesh and blood.

From the *"Our Father,"* in which we claim relationship, right on to *"the kingdom, and the power, and the glory"* (Matthew 6:9, 13), which we ascribe to the only true God, every sentence of **prayer honors the Most High**. The groans and tears of humble petitioners are as truly acceptable as the continual *"Holy, holy, holy"* (Isaiah 6:3) of the cherubim and seraphim, for in their very essence all truthful confessions of personal fault are but homage paid to the infinite perfection of the Lord of Hosts. More honored is the Lord by our prayers than by the unceasing smoke of the holy incense of the altar which stood before the veil.

Moreover, the act **of prayer teaches us our unworthiness**, which is no small blessing to such proud beings as we are. If God gave us favors without requiring us to pray for them, we would never know how poor we are, but a true prayer is an inventory of wants, a catalog of necessities, an exposure of secret wounds, a revelation of hidden poverty. While it is a petition to divine wealth, it is a confession of our emptiness. I believe that the most healthy state of a Christian is to be always empty and always dependent on the Lord for supplies; to be always poor in self and rich in Jesus; to be as weak as water personally, but mighty through God to do great exploits. Hence, the exercise of prayer, while it adores God, lays the creature where he should be—in the very dust.

Prayer is in itself, apart from the answer which it brings, **a great benefit** to the Christian. As the runner gains strength for the race by daily exercise, so for the great race of life, we acquire energy by the sacred labor of prayer. Prayer plumes the wings of God's young eaglets, so that they may learn to mount above the clouds. Prayer girds the loins of God's warriors and sends them forth to combat with their sinews braced and their muscles firm. An earnest pleader comes out of his closet, rejoicing like a strong man ready to run his race. Prayer is that uplifted hand of Moses which routs the Amalekites more than the sword of Joshua. It is the arrow shot from the chamber of the prophet, foreboding defeat to the Syrians. Prayer clothes the believer with the attributes of Deity, girds human weakness with divine strength, turns human folly into heavenly wisdom, and gives to troubled mortals the serenity of the immortal God. Thank You, Lord, for the mercy seat, a choice gift of Your marvelous loving-kindness. Help us to use it rightly.

Just as many mercies are conveyed from heaven in the ship of prayer, so there are many choice, special favors which can only be brought to us by the fleets of unified prayer. God will give to his lonely Elijahs and Daniels many good things, but if *"two of you on earth shall agree as touching anything that they shall ask"* (Matthew 18:19), there is no limit to God's bountiful answers. Peter might never have been freed from prison if it had not been that prayer was made without ceasing by all the church for him. Pentecost might never have come if all the disciples had not been *"with one accord in one place"* (Acts 2:1), waiting for the descent of the tongues of fire.

God is pleased to give many mercies to one intercessor, but at times He seems to say, "You shall all appear before Me and entreat My favor, for I will not see your face unless even your younger brothers and sisters are with you." Why is this, dear friends? I take it that thus our gracious Lord sets forth His **esteem for the communion of the saints**. "I believe in the communion of saints" is one article of the great Christian creed, but how few there are who understand it. There is such a thing as real union among God's people. We may be called by different names, "But all the servants of our King, in heaven and earth are one."

We cannot afford to lose **the help and love of our Christian family**. Augustine said, "The poor are made for the rich, and the rich are made for the poor." I do not doubt that strong saints are made for weak saints, and that the weak saints bring special benedictions upon the full-grown believers. There is a fitness in the whole body. Each joint owes something to every other, and the whole body is bound together and compacted by that which every joint supplies. There are certain glands in the human body which the anatomist hardly understands. He can say of the pancreas, for instance, that it yields a very valuable fluid of the utmost worth in the bodily economy, but there are other secretions whose distinct value he cannot ascertain. However, if that gland were removed, the whole body might doubtless suffer to a high degree.

Likewise, beloved, there may be some believers of whom we may say, "I do not know the purpose for them. I cannot tell what good that Christian does." Yet were that insignificant and apparently useless member removed, the whole body might be made to suffer, the whole frame might become sick, and the whole heart faint. Probably this is the reason why many a weighty gift of heaven's love is only granted to combined petitioning: so that **we may perceive the use of the whole body** and may be compelled to recognize the real vital union which divine grace has made and daily maintains among the people of God.

Is it not a happy thought, dear friends, that the very poorest and most obscure church member can add something to the body's strength? We cannot all preach, we cannot all rule, we cannot all give gold and silver, but we can all contribute our prayers. There is no convert, even though he may be only two or three days old in grace, who cannot pray. There is no bedridden sister in Jesus who cannot pray. There is no sick, aged, imbecilic, obscure, illiterate, or penniless believer who cannot add his supplications to the general stock. This is the church's riches. We put boxes at the door or pass the offering baskets so that we may receive your offerings for God's cause. Remember there is a spiritual chest within the church, into which we should all drop our loving intercessions, as into the treasury of the Lord. Even the widow without her two mites can give her offering to this treasury.

See, then, dear friends, what union and communion there are among the people of God, since there are **certain mercies which are only bestowed when the saints unitedly pray**. How we ought to feel this bond of union and pray for one another! How, as often as the church meets together for prayer and supplication, we should all make it our bound duty to be there! Those of you who are absent from the prayer meetings for any little excuse need to reflect how much you rob the whole body. The prayer meeting is an invaluable institution, ministering strength to all other meetings and ministries. Are there many of you who might, by a little managing of your time and compressing of your labors, be able to attend more often? What if you should lose a customer, do you not think that this loss could be well made up to you by your gains on other days? Even if the loss were not made up, would not the spiritual profit much more than counterbalance any temporal loss? *"Not forgetting the assembling of ourselves together, as the manner of some is"* (Hebrews 10:25).

We are now prepared for a further observation. This **united prayer should especially be made for the ministers of God**. It is for them particularly that this public prayer is intended. Paul asks for it, *"Brethren, pray for us"* (2 Thessalonians 3:1). All God's ministers to the end of time will ever confess that this is the secret source of their strength. The prayers of the people must be the might of the ministers. Shall I try to show you why the minister more than any other man in the church needs the earnest prayers of the people? Is not his position the most perilous? Satan's orders to the hosts of hell are, *"Fight neither with small nor great, save only with the king* [ministers of God]" (1 Kings 22:31). He knows if he can once smite one of these through the heart, there will be a general confusion, for if the champion is dead, then the people flee. It is around the standard-bearer that the fight is heaviest. There the battle-axes ring upon the helmets, and the arrows are bent upon the armor. The enemy knows that if he can cut down the standard or split open the skull of its bearer, he will strike a heavy blow and cause deep discouragement.

Press around us, men at arms! Knights of the red cross, rally for our defense, for the fight grows hot. We urge you that if you elected us to the office of the ministry, stand fast at our sides in our hourly conflicts. I noticed on returning from Rotterdam, when we were crossing the sandbar at the mouth of the Maas, where by reason of a neap tide and a bad wind the navigation was exceedingly dangerous, that orders were issued, "All hands on deck!" I think the life of a minister is so perilous that I may well cry, "All hands on deck. Every man to prayer." Let even the weakest saint become instant in supplication.

Moreover, the minister, standing in such a **perilous position**, has a solemn **weight of responsibility** resting on him. Every man should be his brother's keeper in a measure, but woe to the watchmen of God if they are not faithful, for at their hands will the blood of souls be required. At their door will God lay the ruin of men if they preach not the Gospel fully and faithfully. There are times when this burden of the Lord weighs upon God's ministers until they cry out in pain as if their hearts would burst with anguish.

As the vessel crossed that sandbar, I noted the captain himself was pitching the lead into the sea. When someone asked why he did not let the sailors do it, he said, "At this point, just now, I dare not trust any man but myself to throw the lead, for we have barely six inches between our ship and the bottom." Indeed, we felt the vessel touch once or twice most unpleasantly. So there will come times with every preacher of the Gospel, if he is what he should be, when he will be in anguish for his hearers and will not be able to discharge his duty by proxy, but must personally labor for men's eternal destinies. He will not even trust himself to preach, but calls on God for help since he is now overwhelmed with the burden of men's souls. Do pray for us. If God gives us to you, and if you accept the gift most cheerfully, do not so despise both God and us as to leave us penniless and poverty-stricken because your prayers have been withheld.

Moreover, the **preservation of the minister** is one of the most important objectives for the church. You may lose a sailor from the ship, and that is very bad, both for him and for you. However, if the pilot should fall over, or the captain suddenly become ill, or the helmsman be washed from the wheel, then what does the vessel do? Thus, though prayer is to be put up for every person in the church, yet for the minister is it to be offered first and foremost, because of the position he occupies.

Remember how much more is asked of him than of you. If you are to keep a private table for individual instruction, he is, as it were, to keep a public table as a feast of good things for all comers. How will he do this unless his Master gives him rich provisions? You are to shine as a candle in a house; the minister has to be as a lighthouse to be seen far across the deep. How will he shine the whole night long unless he is trimmed by his Master and fresh oil is given him from heaven? His influence is wider than yours: if it is for evil, he will be a deadly upas tree, with spreading boughs poisoning all beneath his shadow. But if God makes him a star, his ray of light will cheer whole nations and whole periods of time with its genial influence. If there is any truth in this, I implore you to yield your minister generously and constantly the aid of your prayers.

In the original, the word for *"helping together"* implies **very earnest work**. Some people's prayers have no effort in them, but the prayer that prevails with God is a real working-man's prayer in which the petitioner, like Samson, shakes the gates of mercy and labors to pull them up, rather than be denied an entrance. We do not want fingertip prayers, which only touch the burden; we need shoulder prayers, which bear a load of earnestness and are not to be denied their desire. We do not want those dainty runaway knocks at the door of mercy which some give when they show off at prayer meetings, but we ask for the knocking of a man who means to have his petition granted, and means to stay at mercy's gate until it opens and all his needs are supplied.

The **energetic vehemence of the man who is not to be denied**, but intends to take heaven by storm until he wins his heart's desire is the prayer which ministers covet of their people. Melancthon derived great comfort from the information that certain poor weavers, women and children, had met together to pray for the Reformation. For Melancthon, that was solid ground for comfort. Depend on it, it was not Luther only, but the thousands of poor persons who sang psalms behind the plow and the hundreds of serving men and women who interceded that made the Reformation what it was. We are told about Paulus Phagius, a celebrated Hebrew scholar who helped to introduce the Reformation into England, that his most frequent request of his young scholars was that they would continue in prayer so that God might answer by pouring out a blessing.

I have repeatedly said that all the blessing God has given, all the increase in Metropolitan Tabernacle, has been due, under God, to the earnest, fervent prayers of the saints. There have been heaven-moving seasons in this local body. We have had times when we have felt we would die sooner than not be heard, when we have carried our church on our bosom as a mother with her child, when we felt a yearning and a travailing in birth for men's souls. *"What hath God wrought!"* (Numbers 23:23), we may truly say when we see our church daily increasing and the multitudes hanging on our words to hear the Gospel. Should we now cease from prayer? Should we say to the Great High Priest, "Enough"? Should we now pluck the glowing coals from the altar and quench the burning incense? Should we now refuse to bring the morning and evening lambs of prayer and praise to the sacrifice?

Children of God, being armed and carrying bows, will you turn your backs in the day of battle for your church? The flood waters are divided before you. The Jordan is driven back. Will you refuse to march through the depths? Your God goes before you. The shout of a King is heard in the midst of your hosts. Will you now be cowardly and refuse to go up to possess the land? Will you now lose your first love? Will *"Ichabod"* be written on the forefront of your church? Will it be said that God has forsaken you? If not, return to your knees, with all the force of prayer! If not, begin your vehement supplications once more! If not—if you would not see good blighted and evil triumphant—clasp hands, and in the name of Him who ever lives to intercede, be prevalent in prayer that the blessing may descend right where you are. *"Ye also helping together by prayer for us."*

We must now urge you to praise. **Praise should always follow answered prayer.** The mist of earth's gratitude should rise as the sun of heaven's love warms the ground. Has the Lord been gracious to you and inclined His ear to the voice of your supplication? Then praise Him as long as you live. Deny not a song to Him who has answered your prayer and given you the desire of your heart. To be silent over God's mercies is to incur the guilt of shocking ingratitude, and ingratitude is one of the worst of crimes. I trust, dear friends, you will not act as basely as the nine lepers who, after they had been healed of their leprosy, did not return to give thanks to the healing Lord.

To forget to praise God is to refuse to benefit ourselves, for praise, like prayer, is exceedingly useful to the spiritual man. It is a **high and healthy exercise**. To dance like David before the Lord is to quicken the blood in the veins and make the pulse beat at a healthier rate. Praise gives to us a great feast, like that of Solomon, who gave to every man a good piece of meat and a flagon of wine.

Praise is the **most heavenly of Christian duties**. The angels do not pray, but they do not cease to praise both day and night. (See Revelation 4:8.) To bless God for mercies received is to benefit our fellow men, *"the humble shall hear thereof and be glad"* (Psalm 34:2). Others who have been in like circumstances will take comfort when we say, *"Oh! magnify the LORD with me, and let us exalt his name together ...This poor man cried, and the LORD heard him, and saved him out of all his* *troubles*" (Psalm 34:3,6). Tongue-tied Christians are a sad dishonor to the church. We have some whom the devil has gagged, and the loudest music they ever make is when they are champing the bit of their silence. I desire in all such cases that their tongues may sing.

Let us go a step further. As praise is good and pleasant, blessing man and glorifying God, **united praise is especially commendable**. Unified praise is like music in concert. The sound of one instrument is exceeding sweet, but when hundreds of instruments, both wind and stringed, are all combined, then the orchestra sends forth a noble volume of harmony. The praise of one Christian is accepted before God as a grain of incense, but the praise of many is like a censer full of frankincense, wafting its smoke before the Lord. **Combined praise is an anticipation of heaven**, for in that general assembly they altogether with one heart and voice praise the Lord.

> "Ten thousand are their tongues,
>   But all their joys are one."

Public praise is very agreeable to the Christian himself. How many burdens has it removed? I am sure when I hear the shout of praise, it warms my heart. It is at times a little too slow for my taste, and I must urge you to quicken your tempo, so that the rolling waves of majestic praise may display their full force.

Yet with all drawbacks, to my heart there is no music like I hear in the local congregation. My Dutch friends praise the Lord so very slowly that one might very well go to sleep, lulled by their lengthened strains. Even there, however, the many voices make a grand harmony of praise. I love to hear God's people sing when they really do sing, not when it is somewhere between harmony and discord. O for a sacred song, a shout of lofty praise in which every person's soul beats the time, every man's tongue sounds the tune, and each singer feels a high ambition to excel his fellow in gratitude and love! There is something exceedingly delightful in the union of true hearts in the worship of God. When these hearts are expressed in song, sweet are the charming sounds.

I think the church ought to have a praise meeting once a week. We have prayer meetings at least one evening a week, and many have prayer meetings every morning, but why do we not have praise meetings? Seasons should be set apart for services made up of praise from beginning to end. Let us try the plan at once.

As I said that unified prayer should be offered specially for ministers, so should united praise take the same direction: **the whole company should praise and bless God for the mercy rendered to the church through its pastors**. Hear how the apostle Paul puts it again, *"That for the gift bestowed upon us by the means of many persons, thanks* *may be given by many on our behalf.*" Beloved, we ought to praise God for good ministers that they live, for when they die much of their work dies with them. It is astonishing how a reformation will press on while Luther and Calvin live, and how it will cease directly when the reformers die. The spirits of good men are immortal only in a sense. The churches of God in this age are like the Israelites in the times of the judges: when the judges died, they went after graven images again. So it is now, too. While God spares the pastor, the church prospers, but when the man dies, the zeal which he blew to a flame smolders among the ashes. In nine cases out of ten, if not in ninety-nine out of every hundred, the prosperity of a church rests on the minister's life. God so ordains it to humble us. There should be gratitude, then, for **spared life of your pastor**.

We should also have great gratitude for **preserved character**, because when a minister falls, what a disgrace it is! When you read in the news reports the sad case of the Rev. Mr. So-and-So who chose to call himself a Baptist minister, everybody says, "What a shocking thing! What a bad lot those Baptists must be." Now, any fool in the world may call himself a Baptist minister. Our liberty is so complete that no law or order exists. Any man who can get a dozen to hear him is a minister at least to them. Therefore you can suppose that there may be some hypocrites who will take the name in order to get some sort of reputation. If the true minister is kept and made to hold fast to his integrity, there should be constant gratitude to God on his behalf.

If the minister is **well supplied with good material**, if he is like a springing well, if God gives him to bring forth from His treasury things both new and old to feed the people, there should be hearty thanks. If the pastor is kept sound, if he does not go aside to philosophy on the one hand, nor to a narrowness of doctrine on the other, there should be thanksgiving for it. If God gives to the masses the will to hear the teachings, and above all if souls are converted and saints are edified, there should be never-ceasing honor and praise to God.

I am referring now to what you know, and you are just giving mental agreement, but do not think there is much to it. However, if you were made to live in Holland these days for even a short time, you would soon appreciate these remarks. While traveling there, I stayed in houses with godly men, men of God with whom I could hold sweet communion who cannot attend what was once their place of worship. Why not? "Sir," they say, "how can I go to a place of worship when most of the ministers deny every word of Scripture—not only those of the Reformed church, but of every sect in Holland? How can I listen to the traitors who swear to the Calvinistic or Lutheran articles, and then go into the pulpit and deny the reality of the resurrection, or assert that the ascension of Jesus is a mere spiritual parable?"

In the Netherlands, they are fifty years in advance of us in infidelity. We will soon catch up with them if men of a certain school are allowed to multiply. The Dutch ministers have taken great strides in advancing Neologianism, to the point that the people who love the truth (and there are multitudes who are willing to hear it) are absolutely compelled to refuse to go to church at all, lest by their presence they imply their assent to the heretical and false doctrines which are preached every Sunday.

If God were once to take away from England the ministers who preach the Gospel boldly and plainly, you would cry to God to give you the candlestick back again. We may indeed say of England, "With all thy faults, I love thee still." We have a few men of all denominations who are sliding from the truth, but they are nothing as yet. They are a drop in a bucket compared to the churches of Christ. Those among us who are not as Calvinistic as we wish, however, never dispute the inspiration of Scripture nor doubt the truth of justification by faith. We still have faithful men who preach the whole truth of the Gospel.

Be thankful for your ministers. If you were placed where some believers are, you would cry out to God, "Lord, send us back your prophets. Send us a famine of bread or of water, but send us not a famine of the Word!"

I praise God for the help He bestowed on me in the very arduous work in Holland from which I just returned. Praise be to God for the acceptance which He gave me in that country among all of the people. I speak to His praise, and not to mine, for this has been a vow with me: that if God would give a harvest, I would not have an ear of corn of it, but He would have it all. I found in all the places where I went great multitudes of people; crowds who could not understand the preacher, but who wanted to see my face, because God had blessed translated sermons which I had delivered to their souls; many who gave me the grip of brotherly kindness, and, with tears in their eyes, invoked in the Dutch language every blessing upon my head. I had hoped to preach to some fifties and hundreds. Instead of that there were so many that the great cathedrals were not too large. This surprised me and made me glad, and caused me to rejoice in God.

I thank God for the acceptance which He gave me among all ranks of the people. While the poor crowded to shake hands until they almost pulled me in pieces, it pleased God to move the heart of the Queen of Holland to send for me. For over an hour, I was privileged to talk with her concerning the things which make for our peace. I sought no interview with her, but it was her own wish. Then I lifted up my soul to God that I might talk of nothing but Christ and might preach to her of nothing but

Jesus. So it pleased the Master to help me, and I left that very amiable lady, not having shunned to declare the whole counsel of God.

Gratified was I indeed to find myself received cordially by all denominations, so that on the Saturday in Amsterdam, I preached in the Mennonite church in the morning and at the Old Dutch Reformed church in the evening. The next Sunday morning I was in the English Presbyterian church, and then again in the evening in the Dutch Free church. When I sometimes spoke in the great cathedrals, not only were the poor in attendance, but the nobility and the gentry of the land, who could understand English better than most of the poor, who have had no opportunity to learn it.

While going from town to town, I felt the Master helping me continually to preach. I never knew such elasticity of spirit, such an abounding of heart in my life before. I came back, not wearied and tired, though preaching twice every day, but fuller of strength and vigor than when I first set out. I give God the glory for the many souls who have been converted through the reading of the printed sermons, and for the loving blessings of those who followed us to the ship with many tears, saying to us, *"Do thy diligence to come again before winter"* (2 Timothy 4:21), and urging us once more to preach the Word in that land.

There may be mingled with this some touch of egotism. The Lord knows whether it is so or not, but I am not conscious of it. I do bless His name, that in a land where there is so much philosophy, He helped me to preach the truth so simply that I never uttered a word as a mere doctrinalist, but preached Christ and nothing but Christ. Rejoice with me, dear ones. If you will not, I must rejoice alone, but any loaf of praise is too great for me to eat it all.

I need to urge **the joyful claims** which the apostle Paul gives in the twelfth verse, as a reason why there should be prayer and praise for your minister as well as for me. *"For our rejoicing is this, the testimony of our conscience, that in simplicity and godly sincerity, not with fleshly wisdom, but by the grace of God, we have had our conversation in the world, and more abundantly to you-ward."* After all, a man's comfort must come, next to the finished salvation of God, from the testimony of his own conscience. To a minister, what a testimony it is that he has preached the Gospel in simplicity. There are two aspects to **preaching with simplicity**: preaching not with double-mindedness, saying one thing and meaning another; preaching not as oarsmen row, looking one way and pulling another; but rather preaching, meaning exactly what is said, having a single heart, desiring God's glory and the salvation of men. And what a blessing it is to have preached the Gospel simply—without hard words, without polished phrases, never studying elocutionary graces, never straining after oratorical embellishments. How accursed must be the life of a man who pollutes the pulpit with the dignity of eloquence. How desperate will be his deathbed, when he remembers that he made an exhibition of his powers of speech rather than of the solid things which make for winning souls. The conscience that can speak of having dealt with God's truth in simplicity will rest easy.

Paul said, also, that he had preached the Gospel **with sincerity**—that is, he preached as he meant and felt it, preached it so that none could accuse him of being false. The Greek word has a hint in it of sunlight. He is the true minister of God who preaches what he would wish to have displayed in the sunlight, or who has the sunlight shining right through him. I am afraid none of us are like clear glass—most of us are colored a little—but he is happy who seeks to get rid of the tinted matter as much as possible, so that the light of the Gospel may shine straight through him as it comes from the Sun of Righteousness.

Paul had preached with simplicity and sincerity, and he added, *"Not with fleshly wisdom."* Oh, the stories I have heard of what fleshly wisdom will do! I have learned a valuable lesson during the last two weeks which I wish England would learn. There are three schools of theological error in Holland. Each one leaps over the back of its fellow: some of them hold that the facts of Scripture are only myths; others of them say that there are some good things in the Bible, though there are a great many mistakes; and others go further still and fling the whole Bible away altogether as to its inspiration, even though they still preach it and lean on it, saying that they do so only for the edification of the uneducated, merely holding it up for the sake of the common masses (though I ought to add, merely to get their living, as well). How sad that the church has gone to such a length as that—the Old Dutch Reformed church, the very mirror of Calvinism, standing fast and firm in its creeds to all the doctrines we love, and yet gone astray to latitudinous and licentious liberty. How earnestly we decry fleshly wisdom!

I am afraid, dear friends, that some of you, when you hear a minister, want him to express the message well. You find fault unless he shows some degree of talent. I wonder whether that is not a sin? I am half inclined to think it is. I sometimes think whether we ought to look less and less to talent, and more and more to the matter of the Gospel that is preached; whether it is a weakness if we are profited more by a man who is blessed with great elocutionary power; whether we revert back to the days of fishermen and give men no sort of education whatever, but just send them to preach the truth simply, rather than go the present lengths of giving men all sorts of learning that is of no earthly use to them, but which only helps them to pervert the simplicity of God. I love that word in this text, *"Not with fleshly wisdom."*

And now I lay my claim, as my conscience bears me witness—I lay my claim to this same boasting of the apostle Paul. I have preached God's Gospel in simplicity. I have preached it sincerely—the Searcher of all hearts knows that. I have not preached it with fleshly wisdom for one excellent reason: I have not any wisdom of my own and have been compelled to keep to the simple testimony of the Lord. But if I have done anything, it has been done by the grace of God. If any success has been achieved, it has been grace that has done it all.

"And more especially to you-ward." Though our word has gone forth to many lands and our testimony belts the globe, yet *"more especially to you-ward"* has your pastor's ministry been directed. You have we warned; you have we entreated; you have we exhorted; with you have we pleaded; over you have we wept; for you have we prayed. To some of you we have been a spiritual parent in Christ; to many of you as a nursing father; to many of you as a teacher and an edifier in the Gospel; and, we hope, to all of you a sincere friend in Christ Jesus. Therefore, I claim your prayers for your pastor. Though there will be many who remember us in their prayers, I exhort you, inasmuch as our efforts have been *"especially to you-ward,"* let us especially have your prayers.

Some will say that it is unkind of me to suppose that you do not pray. I do not suppose it out of unkindness, but know that some forget to intercede and thank God for us. Continue to pray for us! Rejoice that the Lord has given us to you for your edification and exhortation!

Your whole congregation is not saved yet. There are some that hear us that are not yet converted. Plead with God for their sakes. There are some hard hearts unbroken; ask God to make the hammer strike. While there are some still unmelted, pray to God that He would make the Word like a fire. Pray for your ministers, that God may make them mighty. The church needs still more of the loud voice of God to wake it from its sleep. Ask God to bless all His appointed servants. Energetically plead with Him that His kingdom may come, and His will may be done on earth as it is in heaven.

I pray that all of you will believe in Jesus, for until you do, you cannot pray or praise! O that you all believed in Jesus! Remember this is the only way of salvation. Trust Jesus, *for "he that believeth on him is not condemned: but he that believeth not is condemned already, because he hath not believed in the name of the only begotten Son of God"* (John 3:18). Trust Jesus and you will be saved. May Christ accept you now, for His own love's sake. Amen.

Chapter 6

A Life-long Occupation

"By him therefore let us offer the sacrifice of praise to God continually, that is, the fruit of our lips giving thanks to his name."
—Hebrews 13:15

It is instructive to notice where this verse stands in the whole passage. The connection is a golden setting to this gem of the text. Here we have a description of the believer's position before God. He is finished with all carnal ordinances and has no interest in the ceremonies of the Mosaic law. As believers in Jesus, who is the substance of all the outward types, we have no more to do with altars of gold or of stone. Our worship is spiritual, as well as our altar:

"We rear no altar, Christ has died;
We deck no priestly shrine."

What then? Are we to offer no sacrifice? Far from it. We are called upon to offer to God a continual sacrifice. Instead of presenting in the morning and evening a sacrifice of lambs, and on certain holy days bringing bullocks and sheep to be slain, we are to present to God continually the sacrifice of praise. Having done with the outward, we now give ourselves entirely to the inward and to the spiritual. Do you see your calling, beloved?

Moreover, the believer is now, if he is where he ought to be, like his Master, *"without the camp."* *"Let us go forth therefore unto him without the camp, bearing his reproach"* (Hebrews 13:13). What then? If we are outside the camp, have we nothing to do? Are we cut off from God as well as from men? Shall we fume and fret because we are not of the world? On the contrary, let us ardently pursue higher objects and yield up our disentangled spirits to the praise and glory of God.

Do we come under contempt, as the Master did? Is it so, that we *are "bearing his reproach"*? Shall we sit down in despair? Will we be crushed beneath this burden? No, truly while we lose honor ourselves, we will ascribe honor to our God. We will count it all joy that we are counted worthy to be reproached for Christ's sake. Let us now praise God continually. Let the fruit of our lips be a still bolder confession of His name. Let us more and more earnestly make known His glory and His grace. If reproach is bitter, praise is sweet. We will drown the drops of gall in a sea of honey. If to have our name cast out as evil should seem to be derogatory to us, let us all the more see to it that we give the Lord the glory due His name. While the enemy reproaches us continually, our only reply should be to offer the sacrifice of praise continually to the Lord our God.

Moreover, the apostle says that *"here we have no continuing city"* (Hebrews 13:14). Well, then, we will transfer the continuance from the city to the praise: *"Let us offer the sacrifice of praise to God continually."* If everything here is going, let it go; but we will not cease to sing. If the end of all things is at hand, let them end; but our praises of the living God will abide world without end. Set free from all the hampering effects of citizenship here below, we will begin the employment of citizens of heaven. It is not ours to arrange a new socialism, nor to be dividers of inheritances. We belong to a kingdom which is not of this world, a city of God eternal in the heavens. It is not ours to pursue the dreams of politicians, but to offer the sacrifices of God-ordained priests. As we are not of this world, it is ours to seek the world to come and press forward to the place where the saints in Christ will reign forever.

You see then, beloved, that the text is rather an unexpected one in its connection. But when properly viewed, it is the fittest that could be. The more we are made to feel that we are strangers in a strange land, the more we should addict ourselves to the praises of God with whom we sojourn. Crucified to the world, and the world crucified to us, let us spend and be spent in the praises of Him who is our sole trust and joy. Oh, to praise God continually and never to be put off from praising Him, whatever the world may do!

My great business is to stir you up, dear friends, as many of you as have been made kings and priests unto God by Jesus Christ, to exercise your holy office. To that end, I will first, concerning the Christian, **describe the sacrifice**; secondly, **examine its substance**; thirdly, recommend its exercise; and last**, urge its commencement** at once.

First, concerning a believer, let me describe his sacrifice. *"By him therefore."* At the very threshold of all offering of sacrifice to God, **we begin with Christ**. We cannot go a step without Jesus. Without a Mediator we can make no advance to God. Apart from Christ there is no acceptable prayer, no pleasing sacrifice of any sort. *"By him therefore"* we cannot move a lip acceptably without Him who *"suffered without the gate"* (Hebrews 13:12).

The High Priest of our profession meets us at the sanctuary door. We place our sacrifices into His hands, so that He may present them for us. You would not wish it to be otherwise, I am sure. If you could do anything without Him, you would feel afraid to do it. You only feel safe when He is with you, and you are *"accepted in the beloved"* (Ephesians 1:6). Be thankful that at the beginning of your holy service, your eyes are turned towards our Lord. You are to offer continual sacrifice, looking to Jesus. Behold our great Melchizedek meets us! Let us give Him tithes of all and receive His blessing, which will repay us a thousandfold. Let us never venture upon a sacrifice apart from Him, lest it be the sacrifice of Cain or the sacrifice of fools. He is that altar which sanctifies both gift and giver; **therefore let our sacrifices both of praise and of almsgiving be presented unto God by Him**.

Next, observe that this sacrifice is to be **presented continually**. *"By him therefore let us offer the sacrifice of praise to God continually."* Attentively treasure that word. It will not do for you to say, "We have been exhorted to praise God on the Sabbath." No, I have not exhorted you to such occasional duty. The text says, *"continually,"* and that means seven days a week. I would not have you say, "He means that we are to praise God in the morning when we awake, and in the evening before we fall asleep." Of course, do that unfailingly. But that is not what I have to set before you.

"Let us offer the sacrifice of praise to God continually"—that is to say, without ceasing. Let us make an analogy to that which says, *"pray without ceasing"* (1 Thessalonians 5:17), and say, "[praise] *without ceasing.*" Not only in this place or that place, but in every place, we are to praise the Lord our God. Not only when

we are in a happy frame of mind, but when we are downcast and troubled. The perfumed smoke from the altar of incense is to rise toward heaven both day and night, from the beginning of the year to the year's end. Not only when we are in the assembly of the saints are we to praise God, but when we are called to pass through Vanity Fair, where sinners congregate. *"Bless the Lord at all times"* (Psalm 34:1). Offer the sacrifice of praise to God not just alone in your secret chamber, which is fragrant with the perfume of your communion with God, but in the field, there in the street, and in the hurry and noise of the exchange.

You cannot always be speaking His praise, but you can always be **living His praise**. The heart once set on praising God will, like the stream which leaps down the mountain's side, continue still to flow in its chosen course. A soul saturated with divine gratitude will continue to give forth the sacred aroma of praise, which will permeate the atmosphere of every place and make itself known to all who have a spiritual nostril to discern sweetness.

No moment can be when it would be right to suspend the praises of God: *"therefore let us offer the sacrifice of praise to God continually."* This should be done, not only by some— pastors, elders, deacons, and special workers— but by all believers. The apostle says, *"Let us."* Thus he calls upon all of us who have any participation in the great sacrifice of Christ to go with Him without the camp, and then and there to stand with Him in our places, and continually offer the sacrifice of praise unto God. You see, then, that the two important points are continually, always through Christ.

Paul goes on to tell us what the sacrifice is—the sacrifice of praise. **Praise is heart worship or adoration.** Adoration is the grandest form of earthly service. We ascribe unto Jehovah, the one living and true God, all honor and glory. When we see His works, when we hear His Word, when we taste His grace, when we mark His providence, when we think upon His name, our spirits bow in the lowliest reverence before Him and magnify Him as the glorious Lord. Let us abide continually in the spirit of adoration, for this is praise in its purest form.

Praise is heart-trust and heart-content with God. **Trust is adoration applied to practical purposes**. Let us go into the world trusting God, believing that He orders all things well, resolving to do everything as He commands for His character and His commandments are not grievous to us. We delight in the Lord as He is pleased to reveal Himself, let that revelation be what it may. We believe not only that God is, but that *"he is a rewarder of all them that diligently seek him"* (Hebrews 11:6). Let us so praise Him that we will not be baffled if our work brings us no immediate recompense, for we are satisfied that He is not unrighteous to forget our work of faith.

Let us praise Him by being **perfectly satisfied** with anything and everything that He does or appoints. Let us take a hallowed delight in Him, and in all that concerns Him. Let Him be to us, *"God,* [our] *exceeding joy"* (Psalm 34:4). Do you know what it is to delight yourselves in God? Then, in that continual satisfaction, offer Him continual praise. Life is no longer sorrowful, even amid sorrow, when God is in it, its soul and crown. It is worthwhile to live the most afflicted and tried life, so long as we know God and taste His love. Let Him do what seems to Him good, so long as He will but be God to us and permit us to call Him our Father and our God.

Praise is heart-enjoyment, **the indulgence of gratitude and wonder**. The Lord has done so much for me that I must praise Him, or feel as if I had a fire shut up within me. I may speak for many of you, for you also are saying, *"'He hath done great things'* (Joel 2:20) for us."* The Lord has favored you greatly. Before the earth was, He chose you and entered into covenant with you. He gave you to His Son and gave His Son to you. He has manifested himself to you as He does not to the world. Even now He breathes a childlike spirit into you, whereby you cry, *"Abba, Father"* (Romans 8:15). Surely you must praise Him! How can you ever satisfy the cravings of your heart if you do not extol Him? Your obligations rise above you as high as the heavens above the earth. The vessel of your soul has foundered in this sea of love and gone down fifty fathoms deep in it. High over its masthead the main ocean of eternal mercy is rolling with its immeasurable billows of grace. You are swallowed up in the fathomless abyss of infinite love. You are absorbed in adoring wonder and affection. Like Leah when Judah was born, you cry, *"Now will I praise the Lord"* (Genesis 29:35).

In addition to this, do you not have the praise of heart-feeling, while within you burns an **intense love for God**? Could you love anyone as you love God? After you have poured out the stream of your love upon the dearest earthly ones, do you not feel you have something more within, which all created vessels could not contain? The heart of man yields love without stint, and the stream is too large for the repository into which it flows, so long as we love a created being. Only the infinite God can ever contain all the love of a loving heart. There is a fitness for the heart and a fullness for its emotions when Jehovah is the heart's one object of love. My God, I love You! You know all things. You know that I love You.

Instead of carping at the Lord because of certain stern truths which we read concerning Him, we are enabled in these to worship Him by **bowing our reason to His revelation**.

That which we cannot understand we nevertheless believe, and believing, we adore. It is not ours to accuse the Almighty, but to submit to Him. We are not His censors, but His servants. We do not legislate, but love. He is good, supremely good in our esteem, and infinitely blessed in our hearts. We do not consider what He ought to be, but we learn what He is, and as such we love and adore Him. Thus have I gone all around the shell of praise, but what it really is each one must discover for himself.

The text evidently deals with **spoken praise**: *"Let us offer the sacrifice of praise to God continually, that is, the fruit of our lips giving thanks to his name,"* or, as the Revised Version has it, *"the fruit of lips which make confession to his name."* So, then, we are to utter the praises of God, and it is not sufficient to feel adoring emotions. The priesthood of believers requires them to praise God with their lips. Should we not sing a great deal more than we do? Psalms and hymns and spiritual songs should abound in our homes. It is our duty to sing as much as possible.

We should **praise as much as we pray**. "I have no voice!" says one. Cultivate it until you have. "But mine is a cracked voice!" Ah, well! It may be cracked to human ears and yet be melodious to God. To Him the music lies in the heart, not in the sound. Praise the Lord with song and psalm. A few godly men whom I have known have gone about the fields and along the roads humming sacred songs continually. These are the troubadours and minstrels of our King. Happy profession! May more of us become such birds of paradise! Hear how the ungodly world pours out its mirth. Often times their song is so silly it is utterly devoid of meaning. Are they not ashamed? Then let us not be ashamed. Children of God, sing the songs of Zion, and let your hearts be joyful before your King. *"Is any merry? let him sing psalms"* (James 5:13).

But if we cannot sing so well or so constantly as we would desire, let us talk. We cannot say that we cannot talk. Perhaps some might be better if they could not talk quite so much. As we can certainly talk continually, let us as continually offer to God the sacrifice of praise by **speaking well of His name**. Talk of all His wondrous works. Let *us "abundantly utter the memory of* [His] *great goodness"* (Psalm 145:7). Let *us "praise the Lord for his goodness, and for his wonderful works to the children of men"* (Psalm 107:8).

Many whom you judge to be irreligious would be greatly interested if you were to relate to them your personal story of God's love to you. But if they are not interested, you are not responsible for that. Only tell it as often as you have opportunity. We charge you, as Jesus did the healed man, *"Go home to thy friends, and tell them how great things the Lord hath done for thee, and hath had compassion on thee"* (Mark 5:19). Speak and speak again for the instruction of others, for the confirmation of those who have faith, and for the routing of the doubts of those who believe not. Tell what God has done for you.

Does not our **conversation** need more flavoring with the praise of God? We put into it too much vinegar of complaint, and forget the sugar of gratitude. This year, when the harvest seems to have been snatched from between the jaws of the destroyer, our friends say, "Well, things look a shade better." I am glad to get them up even as high as that. Hear the general talk, "Things are very bad. Business is dreadful. Trade never was so bad." When I was a boy, things I thought were very bad, never were so bad. I have thought ever since they have been so bad that they could not be worse. Yet somehow people live, and even farmers are not all turned to skin and bone. Surely, we had better mend our talk and speak more brightly and cheerily of what God does for us! How can we offer the sacrifice of praise to God continually if we perpetually rail at His providence? Christian, if you are ever driven to a murmur, let it be only a momentary mistake of weakness, but return to contentment and gratitude which is your proper and acceptable condition. Hear the word of the Lord, which says, *"Neither murmur ye, as some of them also murmured, and were destroyed of the destroyer"* (1 Corinthians 10:10).

Praise means this, that you and I are appointed to **tell forth the goodness of God**. Just as the birds of spring wake up before the sun and begin singing—and all of them singing with all their might—so become the choristers of God. Praise the Lord evermore, even as they do who, with songs and choral symphonies. Day and night, circle His throne rejoicing. This is your holy and privileged office.

"Well," says one, "I cannot force myself to praise." I do not want you to force yourself to it. This **praise is to be natural**. It is called the fruit of the lips. In the book of Hosea, from which the apostle Paul quotes, our version reads, *"the calves of our lips"* (Hosea 14:2). Whether the word is *"calves"* in the Hebrew original or not, is a matter in dispute; but the translators of the Septuagint certainly read it *"fruit,"* and this seems more clear and plain. Paul, in quoting it from the Greek translation, endorsed it as being correct.

These lips of ours must produce fruit. Our words are leaves—how soon they wither! The praise of God is the fruit which can be stored up and presented to the Lord. Fruit is a natural product. It grows without force, the free outcome of the plant. So let praise grow out of your lips at its own sweet will. Let it be as natural to you, as regenerated men and women, to praise God as it seems to be natural to profane men to blaspheme His sacred name.

This **praise is to be sincere and real**. The next verse tells us, *"But to do good and communicate forget not: for with such sacrifices God is well pleased"* (Hebrews 13:16). Doing good is joined with praise to God. Many will give God a torrent of words, but scarcely a drop of true gratitude in the form of substance consecrated. When I am pressed with many cares about the Lord's work, I often wish that some of the congregation would be a little more mindful of its monetary needs. I would be much relieved if those who can spare it would help different portions of our home service. It should be the joy of a Christian to use his substance in his Master's service. When we are in a right state of heart, we do not want anybody to call on us to extract a pledge from us, but we go and ask, "Is there anything that needs help? Is any part of the Lord's business in need?"

I often sigh as I see less prominent ministries left without help, not because friends would not aid if they were pressed to do so, but because there is not a ready mind to look out for opportunities. Yet that ready mind is the very fat of the sacrifice. I long to see everywhere Christian friends who will not wait to be asked, but will make the Lord's business their business by taking in hand a branch of work in the church, or among the poor, or for the spread of the Gospel. Let your gift be an outburst of a free and gracious spirit, which takes delight in showing that it does not praise God in word only, but in deed and in truth. Let us excel in generous gifts. Let us see that everything is provided for in the house of the Lord, and that there is no lack in any quarter. This practical praising of the Lord is the life office of every true believer.

Secondly, let us briefly examine **the substance of this sacrifice**. *"Let us offer the sacrifice of praise to God continually."* To praise God continually will need a childlike faith in Him. You must believe His word, or you will not praise His name. Doubt snaps the harp strings. Questions mar all melody. Trust Him, lean on Him, enjoy Him—you will never praise Him unless you do. Unbelief is the deadly enemy of praise.

Faith must lead you into **personal communion with the Lord**. It is to Him that the praise is offered, and not to our fellowmen. The most beautiful singing in the world, if it is intended for the ears of musical critics, is nothing worthy. Praise is only that which is meant for God. "O my Lord, my song will find You! Every part of my being will have its tribute to sing. I will sing unto the Lord, and unto the Lord alone." You must live in fellowship with God, or you cannot praise Him.

You must have an overflowing content, a **real joy in Him**, also. Brothers and sisters, be sure that you do not lose your joy. If you ever lose the joy of your Christianity, you will lose its power. Do not be satisfied to be a miserable believer. An unhappy believer is a poor creature, but he who is resigned to being so is in a dangerous condition. Depend on it, greater importance is attached to holy happiness than most people think. As you are happy in the Lord, you will be able to praise His name. Rejoice in the Lord, that you may praise Him.

There must also be **a holy earnestness** about this. Praise is called a sacrifice because it is a very sacred and solemn thing. People who came to the altar with their victims came there with the hush of reverence, the trembling of awe. We cannot praise God with levity. He is in heaven, and we are on the earth. He is thrice holy, and we are sinful. We must take off our shoes in lowly reverence and worship with intense adoration, or else He cannot be pleased with our sacrifices. When life is real, life is earnest. It must be both real and earnest when it is spent in the praise of the Almighty.

To praise God continually, you need to cultivate **perpetual gratitude**. Surely it cannot be hard to do that! Remember, every misery averted is a mercy bestowed. Every sin forgiven is a favor granted. Every duty performed is also a grace received. The people of God have an inexhaustible treasury of good things provided for them by the infinite God. For all we should overflow with praise for Him. Let your praises be like the waters of fountains which are abundantly supplied. Let the stream leap to heaven in bursts of enthusiasm. Let it fall to earth again in showers of beneficence. Let it fill the basin of your daily life and run over into the lives of others. Then, in a waterfall of glittering joy, let it still descend.

In order to praise, you will need a deep and **ardent admiration** of the Lord God,. Admire the Father. Think much of His love. Acquaint yourself with His perfections. Admire the Son of God, the altogether lovely One. As you mark His gentleness, self-denial, love, and grace, allow your heart to be wholly enamored of Him. Admire the patience and humility of the Holy Ghost, that He should visit you, dwell in you, and bear with you. It cannot be difficult to the sanctified and instructed heart to be filled with a great admiration of the Lord God. This is the raw material of praise. An intelligent admiration of God, kindled into flame by gratitude and fanned by delight and joy, must ever produce praise. Living in personal relationship with God and trusting Him as a child trusts its father, the soul cannot have difficulty with continually offering the sacrifice of praise to God through Jesus Christ.

Thirdly, I want to **recommend this blessed exercise of praise**. *"Offer the sacrifice of praise to God continually,"* because in so doing, you will discover **your reason for being**. Every creature is happiest when it is doing what it is made for. A bird that is made to fly abroad pines in a cage. An eagle would die in the water, even as a fish that is made to swim perishes on the river's bank. Christians are made to glorify God. We are never in our element until we are praising Him. The happiest moments you have ever spent were those in which you lost sight of everything inferior and bowed before Jehovah's throne with reverent joy and blissful praise. I can say it is so with me, and I do not doubt it is so with you. When your whole soul is full of praise, you have at last reached the goal at which your heart is aiming. Your ship is now in full sail. Your life moves on smoothly and safely. This is the groove along which it was made to slide. Before, you were trying to do what you were not made to do, but now you are at home. Your new nature was fashioned for the praise of God, and it finds rest in doing so. Keep to this work. Do not degrade yourself by less divine employment.

Praise God because **it is His due**. Should Jehovah be left unpraised? Praise is the rent which He asks of us for the enjoyment of all things. Will we be slow to pay? Will a man rob God? When it is such a happy work to give Him His due, will we deny it? It blesses us to bless the Lord. Shall we stint God in the measure of His glory? He does not stint us in His goodness. Come, if you have become sorrowful lately, shake off your gloom, and awake all your instruments of music to praise the Lord! Let not murmuring and complaining be so much as mentioned among His saints. *"Give* *unto the Lord the glory due unto his name"* (Psalm 29:2). Shall not the Lord be praised? Surely the very stones and rocks must break their everlasting silence in indignation if the children of God do not praise His name.

Praise Him continually, for it will **help you in everything else**. A man full of praise is ready for all other holy exercises. Such is my bodily pain and weakness, that I could not force myself to prepare this exhortation if I did not feel that I must urge believers to praise God. I thought that my pain might give emphasis to my words. I do praise the Lord. I must praise Him. It is a duty which I hope to perform in my last moments, with the help of the Holy Spirit. Praise helps me to minister.

Whenever you go to any kind of service, even though it is nothing better than opening the shop and waiting behind the counter, you will do it all the better when you are in the spirit of praise and gratitude. If you are a domestic servant and can praise God continually, you will be a comfort in the house. If you are a master and are surrounded with the troubles of life, if your heart is always blessing the Lord, you will keep up your spirits and will not be sharp and ill-tempered with those around you. Praising the Lord is both meat and medicine. Birds of heaven, strange to say, this singing will plume your wings for flight! The praises of God put wings upon pilgrims' heels, so that they not only run, but fly.

Praise will **preserve us from many evils**. When the heart is full of the praise of God, it does not have time to find fault and grow proudly angry with its fellows. Somebody has said a very nasty thing about us. Well, we will answer him when we have finished the work we have in hand, namely, praising God continually. At present we have a great work to do and cannot come down to wrangle. Self-love and its natural irritations die in the blaze of praise. If you praise God continually, the vexations and troubles of life will be cheerfully borne. Praise makes the happy man a strong man. *"The joy of the Lord is your strength"* (Nehemiah 8:10). Praising God makes us to drink of the brook by the way and lift up our heads. We cannot fear while we can praise. Neither can we be bribed by the world's favor, nor cowed by its frown. Praise makes angels of us. Let us abound in it.

Let us praise God because it will be a **means of usefulness**. I believe that a life spent in God's praise would in itself be a missionary life. That matronly sister who never delivered a sermon, nor even a lecture, in all her days has lived a quiet, happy, useful, loving life. All of her family have learned from her to trust the Lord. Even when she will have passed away, they will feel her influence, for she was the angel of the house. *"Being dead,* [she] *yet speaketh"* (Hebrews 11:4). A praiseful heart is eloquent for God. Mere verbiage, what is it but as autumn leaves, which will be consumed in smothering smoke? But praise is golden fruit to be presented in baskets of silver unto the dresser of the vineyard.

Praise God because **this is what God loves**. Notice how the next verse puts it: *"With such sacrifices God is well pleased."* Would we not do anything and everything to please God? It seems too good to be true that we can impart any pleasure to the ever-blessed One. Yet it is so, for He has declared that He is well-pleased with the praises and the gifts of His children. Therefore let us withhold nothing from our dear Father, our blessed God. Can I please Him? Tell me what it is, I will do it right away. I will not deliberate, but without reservation I make haste. If I deliberate, it will only be in order to make the service twice as large or perform it in more careful style. If I may praise Him, it will be honor, it will be heaven to me.

To close this recommendation, remember that the practice of praise will **equip you for heaven**. A hymn expresses a frequent desire:

> "I would begin the music here
> And so my soul should rise."

You can begin the music here—begin the hallelujahs of glory by praising God here and now. Think of how you will praise Him when you see His face and never sin again. Exceedingly magnify the Lord even now, and rehearse the music of the skies. In glory you may rise to a higher key, but let the song be the same even here. Praise Him! Praise Him more and more! Rise on rounds of praise up the ladder of His glory, until you reach the top and are with Him to praise Him better than ever before. Oh, that our lives may not be broken, but may be all one piece—one psalm, forever rising, verse by verse, into the eternal hallelujahs!

The final point to be learned from the text is this: let us **begin at once**. The verse reads, *"Let us offer the sacrifice of praise continually."* The apostle Paul does not say, "Eventually get to this work, when you are able to give up business and have retired to the country, or perhaps when you are near death." Rather, he says, "Now *'let us offer the sacrifice of praise.'"*

Listen! Who is speaking? Whose voice do I hear? I know. It is the apostle Paul. He says, *"Let us offer the sacrifice of praise!"* Where are you, Paul? His voice sounds from within a low place. I believe he is shut up in a dungeon. Lift up your hand, Paul! I can hear the clanking of chains. Paul cries, *"'Let us offer the sacrifice of praise.'* I, Paul the aged, in prison in Rome, wish you to join with me in a sacrifice of praise to God." We will do so, Paul. We are not in prison, we are not all aged, and none of us are galled with shackles on our wrists. We can join heartily with you in praising God, and we do so. Come, let us praise God.

"Stand up and bless the Lord,
   Ye people of his choice;
Stand up and bless the Lord your God
   With heart and soul and voice."

You have heard Paul's voice, now hear mine. Join with me, and let us offer the sacrifice of praise. As His church and people, we have received great favors from the Lord's hand. Come, let us join together with heart and hand across time and space to bless the name of the Lord and worship joyfully before Him. With words and with gifts, let us offer the sacrifice of praise continually. If I could select you, call upon you by name, and would say, "Come, *let us offer the sacrifice of praise,*'" I am sure many of you would reply, "Ah, if nobody else can praise Him, we can, and we will." Well, well, kindly presume it has been done so far as the outward expression is concerned, but inwardly let us at once offer the sacrifice of praise to God through Jesus Christ.

Let us **stir one another to praise**. Let us spend today, tomorrow, and all the rest of our days in praising God. If we catch one another grumbling a little or coldly silent, let us, in kindness to each other, give the needed rebuke. It will not do to murmur. We must praise the Lord. Just as the leader of an orchestra taps his baton to call all to attention and then to begin playing, so I now arouse and stir you to offer the sacrifice of praise unto the Lord.

The apostle Paul has put us rather in a fix: he **compels us to offer sacrifice**. Did you notice what he said in the tenth verse? *"We have an altar"* (Hebrews 13:10), not a material altar, but a spiritual one. Yet, *"we have an altar."* May the priests of the old law offer sacrifice on it? *"Whereof they have no right to eat that serve the tabernacle."* They ate of the sacrifices laid on the altars of the old law, but they have no right here. Those who keep to ritualistic performances and outward ceremonials have no right here. Yet *"we have an altar."* Brothers and sisters, can we imagine that this altar is given us by the Lord never to be used? Is no sacrifice to be presented on the best of altars? *"We have an altar"*—what then? If we have an altar, do not allow it to be neglected, deserted, unused. It is not for spiders to spin their webs upon. It is not fitting that it should be smothered with the dust of neglect. *"We have an altar."* What then? *"Let us offer the sacrifice of praise to God continually."* Do you not see the force of the argument? Practically obey it.

Beside the altar, we have a High Priest. There is the Lord Jesus Christ, dressed in His robes of glory and beauty, standing within the veil at this moment, ready to present our offerings. Shall He stand there and have nothing to do? What would you think of our great High Priest waiting at the altar with nothing to present which His redeemed had brought to God?

No, *"by him therefore let us offer the sacrifice of praise to God continually."* People of God, bring your praises, your prayers, your thank-offerings, and present them to the Almighty!

If you will read the entire context of the key verse, you may well offer your holy sacrifices, because the passage brings before you many things which should compel you to praise God. Behold your Savior in His passion, offered without the gate! Gaze upon His bleeding wounds, His sacred head so blood-stained, His face so full of anguish, His heart bursting with the agony of sin! Can you see that sight and not worship the Lord God? Behold redemption accomplished, sin pardoned, salvation purchased, hell vanquished, death abolished, and all this achieved by your blessed Lord and Master! Can you see all this and not praise Him? His precious blood is falling on you, making you clean, bringing you near to God, making you acceptable before the infinite holiness of the Most High! Can you see yourself thus favored, and behold the precious blood which did it, and not praise His name?

Away in the distance, seen dimly, perhaps, but yet not doubtfully, behold *"a city that hath foundations, whose builder and maker is God"* (Hebrews 11:10). White-robed, the purified are singing to their golden harps, and you will soon be there. When a few more days or years are passed, you will be among the glorified. A crown and a harp are reserved for you. Will you not begin to praise God and glorify Him for the heaven which is in store for you? With these two sights so wonderfully contrasted—the passion and the paradise, and Jesus in His humiliation and Jesus in His glory—you find yourself a sharer in both these wondrous scenes. Surely if you do not begin to offer the perpetual sacrifice of thanksgiving and praise to God, you must be something harder than stone. May we begin today those praises which will never be suspended throughout eternity!

Oh, that you, who have never praised God before, would begin now! Alas! Some of you have no Christ to praise and no Savior to bless. Yet you need not so abide. By faith you may lay hold upon Jesus, and He then becomes yours. Trust Him, and He will justify your trust. Rest in the Lord, and the Lord will become your rest. When you have trusted, then waste no time, but at once begin the business for which you were created, redeemed, and called. Fill the censor with the sweet spices of gratitude and love, and lay on the burning coals of earnestness and fervency. Then, when praise begins to rise from you like pillars of smoke, swing the censor to and fro in the presence of the Most High, and more and more laud, bless, and magnify the Lord that lives forever. Let your heart dance at the sound of His name, and let your lips show forth His salvation.

May the Lord anoint you this day to the priesthood of praise, for Christ's sake! Amen.